W9-BGN-250

Seeking Solid Ground *provides bricks and mortar for a graced life that will never be shaken.*

R. Kent Hughes
Pastor, College Church
Wheaton, Illinois
Author of *Disciplines of a Godly Man*

John Trent and Rick Hicks give us wise words on how to build an unshakable life in a tremor-filled, fault-lined world. Seeking Solid Ground *is a great book for anyone whose world is not problem-free.*

John Ortberg
Preaching Pastor, Willow Creek Community Church
South Barrington, Illinois

Seeking Solid Ground *is solid gold encouragement mined from one of the finest psalms and refined by two of the greatest thinkers in the church. Each chapter will make your heart grow stronger and your courage run deeper.*

Tim Kimmel
President
Generation Ministries
Author of *How to Deal with Powerful Personalities*

SEEKING
SOLID
GROUND

SEEKING SOLID GROUND

Anchoring Your Life in Godly Character

John Trent, Ph.D.
Rick Hicks, Ph.D.

PUBLISHING
Colorado Springs, Colorado

SEEKING SOLID GROUND

Copyright © 1995 by John Trent and Rick Hicks. All rights reserved. International copyright secured.

ISBN 1-56179-400-7

Published by Focus on the Family Publishing, Colorado Springs, CO 80995. Distributed in the U.S.A. and Canada by Word Books, Dallas, Texas.

Unless otherwise noted, Scripture quotations are from the *New American Standard Bible,* © 1960, 1963, 1968, 1971, 1973, 1975, and 1977 by The Lockman Foundation. Used by permission. Those identified as NIV are from the HOLY BIBLE, NEW INTERNATIONAL VERSION ®. Copyright © 1973, 1978, 1984 by the International Bible Society. Used by permission of Zondervan Publishing House. All rights reserved. Those marked KJV are from the King James Version of the Bible.

People's names and certain details of the case studies in this book have been changed to protect the privacy of the individuals involved. However, the facts of what happened and the underlying principles have been conveyed as accurately as possible.

No part of this publication may be reproduced, stored in a retrieval system, or transmitted in any form or by any means—electronic, mechanical, photocopy, recording, or otherwise—without prior permission of the publisher.

Front cover design: Bradley Lind
Front cover photo: Rich Buzzelli

Printed in the United States of America

95 96 97 98 99/10 9 8 7 6 5 4 3 2 1

To my precious wife, Cindy,
whom God has used to build up the twin pillars
of unconditional love and lifelong commitment
in our nearly 20 years of marriage.
I love you, honey.

John

To Ralph Klages, my father-in-law,
who was the first person, after I became a Christian,
to impress on me the need for a life of integrity
and who served as a role model.
Thanks.

Rick

CONTENTS

Acknowledgments

I (John) would like to express my deepest thanks and appreciation to the team of friends who make up the Encouraging Words board and staff: Bob and Jo Leenhouts, Kevin and Nancy Steele, John and Donna Vryhoff, Dan and Kris Stockfisch, Rich and Linda Simons, Doug and Judy Childress, Don and Nancy Schlander, Jim and Pam McGuire, and Amy Stuber. Thank you all for helping to shoulder the extra load at the ministry and at CrossTrainers while we were finishing this book. Also, special thanks to several other people whom God has used mightily to bless our family these past months: Don and Ruth Rodie, Jay and Christie Abraham, and my faithful family, Zoa Trent, Jeff and Diane Trent, and Joe and Marnel Trent.

I (Rick) would like to thank my wife, Kathy, who was an equal partner with me in writing my portion of this book. Thank you also for standing by me while God taught me (and continues to teach me) character lessons from Psalm 15. Thanks to the Forest Home staff, who have encouraged me during these past few months. A special thanks to Teri

Glass, my dedicated secretary, who, after a full day's work, went home and on her own time typed portions of this book. To my daughter, Cora, I apologize for the missed "dates" and thank you for your patience. Finally, to John Trent: Thank you for allowing me to work with you and for sharing the deep feelings I have about Psalm 15.

Both of us would like to thank those at Focus on the Family with whom we have worked: Al Janssen, Larry Weeden, Lorraine Beck, and the rest of the Book Publishing team. We also thank Mark Wheeler, Steve Lyon, and Dave Hopkins for their insights and contributions in our attempt to convey God's promise of Psalm 15.

THE PATHWAY
TO SOLID GROUND

Chapter 1

Unexpected Tremors

I n certain places, like Southern California or the shores of Japan, people know tremors are coming. You can see the extra "sway" being built into office buildings, watch as they retrofit the overpasses on the freeways, and marvel at the chain of stores springing up in local malls that sell nothing but emergency water and equipment.

Folks there realize that no matter how secure things seem today, a time will come when their lives will be shaken—literally. And as the horrible tragedy in Oklahoma City made painfully clear, the same potential for being shaken holds true for each and every one of us.

For some of us, the shaking comes as a mild jolt or unexpected tremor. For others, it may be major shifts in the layers of their lives, rattling them down to their cores, just as it shook the four people below.

Life Can Shake a Storybook Marriage

Kay couldn't believe the irony of it all. Just a few months earlier, she'd been asked to play a part in a promotional video. The role? That of a single parent struggling to make ends meet with a new job and young kids at home.

At first, it didn't make sense for her to take the part. After all, she was more than happily married and had never had to face the challenges of a single-parent home. But she did have some acting experience, and this was just playing a role. So she agreed to join the cast and help with the project.

Little did Kay know that at the very time she was role-playing a single-parent mom, real forces were taking shape that would turn her fictional role into rock-hard reality. In a move that caught her off guard and unprepared, her marriage came totally unraveled. Less than six months after the video came out, she wasn't just acting the part of a single mom. "Divorce granted." Out of the blue, her world had been shaken.

Life Can Shift a Profession

It wasn't the biggest business going. But after slaving day and night for three years, plowing every red cent back into the business, the Redondo brothers had finally turned the corner. In part, it was because the area near their shop had finally filled in. Now they were on a busy corner nestled among hundreds of new houses and apartments—homes filled with tired workers who were stopping by in droves to buy a "better than homemade" pizza.

But then the letter came from their landlord about that "technicality" they'd overlooked, those two payments they'd made up in full but had been late in making. Suddenly, the Redondo brothers weren't gazing into an exciting future with a lease extension but were staring at eviction instead. A short time later, unable to compete financially in court with their wealthy landlord, they watched as a national chain muscled its way into their location and took over their customers.

Life Can Challenge Convictions

"Just go along," they said. Only three words. But they were given as a command, not as a suggestion. In fact, they came as a life-or-death challenge to Kurt.

In 1975, Kurt was a graduate student working as a bellhop at a prestigious downtown hotel. Major conventions and well-to-do customers made for lucrative tips, a dream come true for the impoverished seminarian. But then came the day he casually mentioned to another bellhop something about filing his taxes—and about how glad he was that he'd kept such good records of his tips.

That's all it took to alert the others that a "good thing" stood in jeopardy. As Kurt ended his shift, he found himself surrounded by several of the other bellhops. If he accurately reported his tips and the IRS discovered what one of them was really making, they said, it could damage those who had been grossly underreporting their incomes.

That's when they made it perfectly clear to Kurt that if he chose to be truthful, his physical well-being would be damaged.

Life Can Collide with Families

It was a beautiful, small-town summer morning. Puffy white clouds dotted the sky, and people were already mowing their lawns and getting their boats ready for the lake.

What lay before Tim that day was a trip to Dallas with the family to visit his in-laws. Marcy already had the girls up and was getting them dressed. All he had to do was buy some donuts for the trip ("high-fiber Frisbees," they called them), fill the car with gas, and—oh, yes. He also had to stop by the pediatrician's office and pick up the results of his kids' annual physicals.

"Hi, Joyce," Tim said with his usual enthusiasm as he walked into the doctor's office. "You and Phil going to the lake this afternoon?"

In a small town, people's habits become well known, and Tim knew that the minute the office closed at noon on Saturday, the receptionist's family would head to their cabin on the lake.

He also was familiar with Joyce's always-present smile . . . which seemed to disappear the minute he walked in the door. "Dan needs to talk with you, Tim," she said without the usual welcome and chitchat. Then she disappeared into the back office.

Talk with me? Tim thought. His heart skipped a beat. *It's probably just something about the church,* he concluded.

That must be it. Tim and his good friend and neighbor Dr. Dan were both on the board of deacons, and they were in the middle of calling that new pastor. Something must have hit a snag.

Walking into the waiting room, Dan, dressed in a stark white coat, said, "Tim, I need to talk to you. Come on back in my office."

Thirty minutes later, Tim walked outside. The heat and humidity were rising, but he felt cold and numb inside. *How am I going to tell Marcy? There have got to be other tests that will prove this is all a mistake. Amy's only seven years old. Lord, she can't have cancer! She can't! We're going on a trip today and a picnic. She's my little Pumpkin. She's got to be okay. Nothing's going to change!*

But change it did. Quickly. Quietly. And for the worse.

Amy fought the cancer with courage and a childlike faith that blessed the community and inspired her parents to hang on through each emotion-packed day. But on Halloween night, her frail little body had had enough. Her ragged breathing stopped, and her head lay still on the pillow. Her battle was over.

Tim and Marcy's had just begun.

Financially, personally, relationally, emotionally, spiritually—none of us gets a "free pass" card when it comes to the potential for our lives to be shaken. And though the scenarios above are certainly dramatic examples, major moves and changes in life are more common than we'd like to admit.

Did We Get the Title Right on This Book?

In a turbulent world, isn't it false advertising to claim that there really is a place of solid security? A way of life that anchors us in biblical bedrock that can help us weather any storm and stay firmly attached to God's best?

Absolutely not!

It was God Himself who promised us a "life that can never be shaken." That promise was penned by one of His best-loved servants, a man who lived his entire life on an active emotional fault line: King David.

In our lives today, the answer to security doesn't lie in "barking dog" alarms and barred windows. Nor is it gained by laughing off the potential threat of change and leaving ourselves and our children unprepared.

When our lives are shaken (and one day they will be), every one of us needs to know how and where to seek solid ground. In the pages that follow, you'll discover that the road map to anchoring our lives is only five verses long.

Sound impossible? Hardly. Those five verses were the first place a wise president looked when his nation had been shaken.

Reflections
Unexpected Tremors

1. Chapter 1 contains the accounts of several people who experienced difficulty in their relationships, marriages, professional life, job security, convictions, families, and emotions. When was the last time you went through a trying experience that shook your life? How did you feel during that period? What did you do to resolve the problem?

2. Rate the level of stability you are currently feeling in the following areas of your life:

	Quake damaged			Tremors					Rock Solid	
friendships	1	2	3	4	5	6	7	8	9	10
marriage	1	2	3	4	5	6	7	8	9	10
family	1	2	3	4	5	6	7	8	9	10
professional life	1	2	3	4	5	6	7	8	9	10
job security	1	2	3	4	5	6	7	8	9	10
convictions	1	2	3	4	5	6	7	8	9	10
emotions	1	2	3	4	5	6	7	8	9	10

3. If you were offered a "road map" that would guarantee that you and your family could find a place of genuine, lifetime security, what would you be willing to pay?

4. At the end of the chapter, it was mentioned that God gave a promise through King David that we would never be shaken. How did you feel when you read that statement? Skeptical? Curious? Disbelieving?

5. Just in case you have any questions about how dependable God's Word is, read these verses: 2 Timothy 3:16; 2 Peter 1:20; Romans 15:4; Matthew 5:18. (For a full buffet to feed your understanding of the benefits of God's Word, read all of Psalm 119.)

 *Chapter 2*

A Rock in
a Hard Place

Have you ever stood in the eye of a storm?

You could have if you'd lived during one of the most dramatic periods in our nation's history. In that time, you could have looked back just five years and stared full-face at the worst economic depression our country has ever experienced. Hundreds of thousands lost their jobs, savings, businesses, and homes. Shelters and shantytowns dotted the landscape, and long lines at soup kitchens were an everyday occurrence, not just holiday exceptions.

A look back would have pictured times of unprecedented economic trials, but if you could have peeked just seven years into the future, you would have seen something even more terrible—the gravestones of nearly 300,000 of your friends, neighbors, fathers, and brothers, each one killed in the worst of world wars. (Millions more soldiers and civilians of all nations died as well.)

Sandwiched between the Great Depression and the Second World War—perhaps the most-trying one-two punch in our country's history—

was an event that occurred on a bright spring day in 1938. March 5, 1938, to be exact.

If ever a nation needed a message of hope and assurance, it was then. People ached for the strength to walk past the economic devastation they'd experienced, and they longed for the fortitude to face the personal, family, and worldwide challenges that lay ahead. That's why they stopped that spring day to listen to one man speak. Actually, it was a voice they'd grown accustomed to hearing each Sunday afternoon on his weekly radio "fireside chats." Yet, on this occasion—the beginning of his sixth year as president—Franklin Delano Roosevelt gave a different kind of speech.

With his country coming out of an economic depression and standing on the brink of world war, Roosevelt had gone to St. John's Episcopal Church that March morning to ask for divine guidance as head of the nation. Stirred by the sermon, Roosevelt said something prophetic at a press conference that followed the service. His opening words startled the reporters (and we're confident that reporters today would have been even more startled). In that trademark voice, he boomed: *"I ask that every newspaper in the country print the text of the Fifteenth Psalm. . . . There could be no better lead for your story."*[1]

With those words, the president pointed not only to the state of our country, but also to something deeper . . . to the state of our souls.

But Psalm 15? Read a *psalm* when there was great need for healing? Publish a *poem* at a time when people were asking challenging questions? Highlight an *ancient song* when economic times were tough and world-wide challenges were mounting?

Exactly!

And if ever a nation needed an echo of that same message, it's today!

Gaining God's Best . . . Preparing for Life's Worst

Historians and politicians may argue over whether Roosevelt's role as the architect of the New Deal was right, but what he did that March day was right on. Those five simple verses, penned by a shepherd turned statesman centuries before, should have been headline news.

They should still be today.

Those verses carry just the right mix of challenge, instruction, reproof, and encouragement to help a nation of weary individuals step away from past hurts and toward a God-honoring future.

Our goal in this book is to give you the chance to discover for yourself, your family, your church, or your small group the incredible power, wisdom, and direction that are packed into this single psalm. It's not just a nice quote that a wise president referred to. It's God's enduring words that can help answer life's most heartfelt questions—and it can help lead you to the true source of healing and hope.

The ten principles God had David put in Psalm 15 are far more valuable than any self-help book could ever be. In fact, what you'll discover is:

- an advanced course in character development
- a graduate curriculum in human relations
- and a cum laude degree in compassion and genuine love.

What's more, they're topped off by an incredible promise from God that He Himself can add an inner layer of emotional concrete—a new sense of security and rest—to your hectic life.

We prayed specifically that you'd pick up this book. We truly believe it wasn't an accident. Perhaps you've gone through your own version of the Great Depression or faced years of inner battles or relational wars.

Whatever your situation, *don't lose heart!*

It doesn't take a strong faith to turn the page and dip your feet into Psalm 15. But for all who will try the water and then take the plunge, we can guarantee that the clear water of the Word will help cleanse, renew, restore, and inspire you to do two things: gain more of God's best . . . and be better prepared for life's worst.

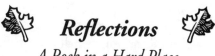

Reflections
A Rock in a Hard Place

1. When have you felt sandwiched between two trials? Where did you turn for help?

2. Did your upbringing teach you how to deal with unexpected changes? If not, how have you learned to cope?

3. If you turned on the radio today and heard the president of the United States tell you to read from the Book of Psalms, how would you respond? Would you consider it mere political rhetoric? Would you consider it to be putting a Band-Aid on cancer? Would you follow his advice and read it? Would you believe the message of the psalm? Would you practice the principles found in the psalm?

4. John and Rick claim that Psalm 15 offers help in character development, human relations, compassion, genuine love, and gaining a new sense of security and rest. Rank your level of satisfaction regarding the presence of those qualities in your life today:

	Complete Absence				Needs Help				Filled to the Brim	
Growth toward maturity	1	2	3	4	5	6	7	8	9	10
Relational ability	1	2	3	4	5	6	7	8	9	10
Compassion	1	2	3	4	5	6	7	8	9	10
Genuine love	1	2	3	4	5	6	7	8	9	10
Feelings of security	1	2	3	4	5	6	7	8	9	10
Sense of rest	1	2	3	4	5	6	7	8	9	10
Emotional satisfaction	1	2	3	4	5	6	7	8	9	10

5. If you were to ask God to help cleanse, renew, restore, and inspire you in one area of your life, what would it be? Why? Why not pray and tell Him that right now (see 1 John 1:9; Ps. 32; Ps. 51)?

Chapter 3

Finding Tangible Help in Tough Times

My (John's) first close look at Psalm 15 came in a class on the Psalms at Dallas Theological Seminary in 1975. It was taught by Dr. Bruce Waltke, a noted Hebrew scholar and a sensitive, godly man. I was struggling to learn Hebrew grammar and syntax, and I have to admit that my major goals were to survive his infamous tests and to avoid being called on in class—not to be personally stretched and sanctified.

What was our first psalm to translate? Psalm 15. As I began to translate the verses, instead of reading ancient history, I felt as if I had grabbed hold of a lit Roman candle! The key words and phrases in that psalm exploded like bright colored balls that shot out and burst forth with meaning and practical application.

For me (Rick), this psalm first grabbed my attention as I was doing the "Evelyn Wood Speed Reading" method of daily devotions one morning. Although I don't remember much about my speed-reading course in college, I do recall someone saying that you read the first and last sentence of a passage and then speed through the rest.

Determined to make it through my devotions in record time that day, I read the first verse of Psalm 15, "Who may abide in Thy tent? Who may dwell on Thy holy hill?" and it slowed me down. Then I read the last verse, and it stopped me cold: "He who does these things will never be shaken."

Forget the speed reading. Those two bookend verses were so powerful and promised so much that I began a 20-year process of teaching, studying, and trying to live out daily what they said.

We're both sold on the fact that God, through King David, centered some of His most life-changing truths in these few short verses—beginning with the positive changes we've seen in our own lives over more than two decades. So, without further ado, let's take our first look at this key passage:

A Psalm of David

> O Lord, who may abide in Thy tent?
> Who may dwell on Thy holy hill?
> He who walks with integrity, and works righteousness,
>   And speaks truth in his heart.
> He does not slander with his tongue,
>   Nor does evil to his neighbor,
> Nor takes up a reproach against his friend;
> In whose eyes a reprobate is despised,
>   But who honors those who fear the Lord;
> He swears to his own hurt, and does not change;
> He does not put out his money at interest,
>   Nor does he take a bribe against the innocent.
> He who does these things will never be shaken.

That's a popular rendering of this timeless passage. However, try reading it again in the Trent-Hicks amplified translation.

A Psalm of David the King

> O Lord, who may be Your traveling companion on earth,
> And dwell forever with You in heaven?
>   *(The answer? In our personal life . . .)*
> It's someone who walks with seamless integrity,

Trusts You for the power to do what's right (even when it's
   difficult),
And strives to tell himself and others the truth.
   (In our important relationships . . .)
It's someone who doesn't gather "inside information" on a
   friend and then twist it with others in order to harm him.
He avoids choices that he knows will harm his neighbor,
   And he refuses to carry a grudge against a good friend.
   (And in our public walk . . .)
It's someone who rejects those who deserve to be rejected,
   But honors those who walk in tight fellowship with Almighty
   God;
He's the type of person who makes a commitment and doesn't
walk away from it;
   Doesn't lend money to those in need at loan-shark rates,
   Nor does he sell out a brother who's done nothing wrong,
   putting money above integrity.
   (And there's a promise from God for those who live such a life.)
He who does these things will never be shaken.

In the pages that follow, we'll focus on each major word and section of
Psalm 15, and we'll give you an opportunity to do four important things.

1. You'll be challenged to give an answer to the most important questions you'll ever be asked.

"Who may abide in Thy tent? Who may dwell on Thy holy hill?"

People clamor to get sideline passes and front-row seats at sporting
events. Lobbyists and high-income supporters spend thousands to rub
shoulders with, or at least sit ten tables away from, a congressman or presi-
dential candidate. Others wait for hours to catch a glimpse of a
Hollywood or Broadway star on opening nights, and a special few even
get backstage passes.

Yet, what does it take to get a sideline pass to walk with the King of
kings? What can we do to be front and center with the Lord of lords who
created the universe? How do we get to go backstage with the Author and
Director of our lives?

Without a doubt, the most important thing we'll ever do is to learn the answer to the questions that open Psalm 15: "Who may abide . . . ? Who may dwell . . . ?" For our answer will determine not only the fullness and quality of our lives today, but also the issue of where we'll spend eternity.

2. You'll discover 10 lifestyle traits that build a life of unshakable inner character.

In the pages that follow, we'll go into detail on each of the 10 traits listed in the verses above. But you'll be challenged to do more than just feed your gray cells. You'll also have the chance to take a self-evaluation exercise that can help you pinpoint how well you're displaying those 10 traits today. What's more, each chapter ends with an opportunity for reflection to help make these principles an active part of your life.

Whether you're a woman who wants to deepen her faith in Christ or a man who's looking to grow in his spiritual life, you'll find practical help in the clear picture David penned of an unshakable life.

3. In these few short verses, you can find a blueprint for being a better parent and a more loving spouse.

Psalm 15 is primarily directed at helping us deepen our faith in Almighty God and helping us develop an unshakable confidence in His goodness and strength. But there's a wonderful sidelight to putting these 10 principles into practice. Namely, they'll help brighten your most important relationships as well. For when it comes to fulfilling our roles as spouses or parents, Psalm 15 can give us a detailed plan for modeling Christ before our loved ones.

If you're confused in applying any of the hundreds of parenting theories and techniques circulating today, we can state without fear of contradiction that Psalm 15 offers unbeatable advice. In terms of developing character (our own and our children's), taking responsibility, and building sensitivity, modeling Psalm 15 will provide lifelong positive effects that can rub off on the next generation.

4. You'll discover the action-oriented promise of an unshakable life.

We haven't said much yet about that last inspiring verse in Psalm 15: "He who does these things will never be shaken." But we've thought much about it. As two men who daily see people whose lives have been tossed and shaken, we can't think of a promise from God Himself that is more needed today. Yet, it's a promise that seems hard to accept because of our experiences.

I (Rick) have to admit that what stopped me cold that first day I really read Psalm 15 was the promise that my life would never be shaken. For me (John), coming from a single-parent home and some challenging situations with my father, the idea of an unshakable life was likewise hard to swallow.

After all, we're both children of the sixties. Our generation became the poster children for cultural upheaval. Remember, we were the ones who questioned everything from Nixon to hairstyles to anyone over age 30. So, when someone promises anything with absolute certainty—much less that we can build an inner center that can never be shaken—well . . .

If such a claim were made today, the next thing you'd hear would be the announcer's voice on fast-forward saying, "Of course, there are exceptions to this promise, so it may or may not be applicable to your particular situation, so don't take this literally. . . . Void where prohibited by law."

But in Psalm 15, the lawyer language never comes! That's because this promise isn't just Madison Avenue hype. It's God's own promise that He can give us a rock-solid quality of life and genuine inner peace that truly creates an unshakable center. And as you'll see, that's not just a promise for saints; it's for us occasional "ain'ts" as well.

Ready to dig into this life-changing passage of Scripture? Good, because in the next chapter, you'll discover four important lessons from the "fine print" at the beginning of Psalm 15. It starts with a word about the author—someone who (from an earthly perspective) should have been the last one chosen to pick up a pen (or stylus) and write such a psalm.

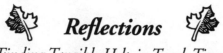

Reflections
Finding Tangible Help in Tough Times

1. Read Psalm 15 twice, once in your favorite translation and once in the Trent-Hicks amplified version on pages 14-15.

2. As we get ready to look at the life of King David, read 1 Samuel, chapters 16 through 31, for a snapshot of his life.

3. What in David's life can you relate to? Being successful? Facing down enemies? Showing compassion? Coming back from sin? Having a heart that truly seeks God?

4. In what areas of life are you most vulnerable to being shaken? Why?

Four Vital Lessons from the Fine Print

For many people, reading the words *background material* creates the same desire that makes us reach for the remote control to fast-forward past the "FBI Warning" at the beginning of a video! Yet, in our look at Psalm 15, these introductory observations aren't optional—they're essential for understanding what follows. What's more, they include several important principles we can take to heart today.

Lessons from Someone Who Doesn't Laugh at Scars

Psalm 15 actually begins *before* the first verse. Set on top of this psalm like a crown is the heading "A Psalm of David." What can we learn from that? Shakespeare has one of his characters in *King Lear* say, "He laughs at scars who himself never bore a wound." Believe us, David wouldn't have laughed.

If you looked throughout Scripture, you'd be hard-pressed to find anyone who took as many blows in life as David. In fact, this herdsman-turned-national hero should have been writing songs about coming apart at the seams instead of never being shaken.

For those who may not be familiar with this favored king, David spent his life at the epicenter of personal and cultural change. In fact, he experienced more highs and lows than an elevator operator at the Sears Tower. Take a look at a short list of some of the twists and turns David experienced.

- He went from courageously standing up to a 10-foot giant to covering up his double sins of adultery and murder.
- He was rewarded for his bravery in battle by getting to marry the king's daughter; later, she mocked him in front of his friends as his marriage ended.
- He had the joy of becoming a parent and the heartbreak of losing a baby. In later years, he even had two of his grown children take up arms and try to overthrow his kingdom and kill him.
- He had a best friend who stood up for him at the risk of his life and fair-weather friends who deserted him at the drop of a hat.

And if you think you've got problems with your employer, David's boss tried to drive a spear through him—twice! David faced decapitation, not just corporate downsizing, as he spent months being hunted like a criminal in the wilderness. Even as a boy, David had faced numerous "shakable" circumstances. While working as a shepherd, he took on a lion and a bear to save his sheep!

David's life was shaken from top to bottom. His days were marked by change, calamity, courage, conviction . . . but never complacency. From falling on his knees in repentance to dancing in the streets after a great victory, David's life was a nonstop roller-coaster ride.

At least that's how it looked on the outside.

On the inside, David had a "center" to his life that never changed, never moved, never was shaken . . .

- no matter how trying or troublesome his circumstances
- no matter how heartfelt his cry, "O Lord, why do You let the wicked triumph?"
- no matter how many times he fell on his own or others tried to push him down
- no matter whether he was a penniless shepherd or the wealthiest king in his part of the world.

In combat, in the throne room of a palace, or hiding in a cave, David always returned to an unshakable, nonslip center. He knew an inner place of rock-solid stability where he could find the honesty to express his hurts and confusion to God ("Why, O Lord?"), yet could always draw on the humble strength to say, "Yet will I trust You."

If you're like us, you need some of that strength. That's because most of us frequently have our lives turned topsy-turvy. And that's why that short heading, "A Psalm of David," carries so much weight.

The 10 anchor points David wrote about come from someone who's been where we've been and, in most cases, faced more than we'll face. In King David, Scripture provides us with a real-life role model for handling personal upheaval and change. And if David found a quiet place amid the storm, we can, too.

Besides pointing out the life and character of the author of Psalm 15, we need to make another observation before we begin studying this psalm in depth. Namely, why are there 10 things set forth as stability points? In fact, why bother with a list at all?

One List You Can't Do Without

Are you one of those people who can't get along without a list? For some of us, our daily list of things to do ranks in sanctity right behind our Bible. The mere thought of losing our lists can cause us to shake as if we've just sworn off morning coffee.

For others, lists are a sign of weakness. For example, I (John) think of one man who was in an accountability group. To start the year, each person in the group wrote down his goals for making positive changes in his life, then handed a copy to each of the other men for prayer and accountability.

Three weeks later, my friend had lost his copy of his own list and had to borrow one from one of the other guys so he could remember what he needed to work on! (Of course, to be honest, his initials are John Trent!)

Some of us lean on lists more than others, but each of us needs the list recorded in this passage. Yet, why a list at all? And why 10 things instead of seven, six, or 101?

For one thing, God *likes* lists! You may not have noticed it, but there are dozens of lists in Scripture.

God listed things He hates and things He loves (see Prov. 6:16–19). The apostle Paul gave us a listing of the "fruit of the Spirit" (see Gal. 5:22–23), and Peter listed the qualities of a mature Christian (see 2 Pet. 1:5–8). There are lists of qualifications for being an elder or deacon, long genealogical lists of who begat whom, lists of people who were examples of faith and failure, and even a list of seven churches that were closely evaluated by the Lord Himself in the Book of Revelation (see 2:1–3:22).

Of all the lists God gave us, one in the Old Testament tops them all. It's called the Decalogue, or the Ten Commandments (see Exod. 20), and Moses received it directly from the finger of God.

Those 10 laws lay out clear boundaries around the behavior of God's people, and they were known to every Hebrew who read or heard Psalm 15. But why 10 fences around our conduct?

Playing Inside the Fence

Several years ago, an interesting study was done of playground behavior in young children.[1] The children came from several different schools, but each school had essentially the same size play area and the same ratio of teachers to students. Yet, there was one major difference between the two types of schools being studied: One group of schools offered children a fenced playground; the other group had a play area with no fence.

When the study was over, guess which students showed more cooperative play, had fewer playground fights, and exhibited lower levels of anxiety during recess? Here's a hint: It was the same group that used more space on the playground and had better attitudes toward schoolwork following recess.

"Easy!" you say. "The kids who played in the wide-open spaces. Right?"

Wrong!

The children who played behind the protective boundaries of a fence were far happier at play and better adjusted after recess. When it comes to playground behavior, children playing inside a fence feel a security that other children do not. And when it comes to grown-up kids living in the fast lane, having "fences" around their behavior is just as important.

God gave us His great Ten Commandments to keep us inside the fences of His love and blessing. Hundreds of years later—by design, not by accident—He gave us another list of 10 fences in Psalm 15.

The parallels between these two great sections of Scripture are striking. In fact, in an ancient commentary on God's Word called the Talmud, we're told, "Of the 613 commandments of the Pentateuch, each is summarized in this Psalm."[2] In other words, these 10 traits of a godly, unshakable lifestyle crystallize God's moral purpose for our lives.

It may seem paradoxical that fences can lead to inner freedom, yet that's just what happens when we stay within God's boundaries. When we adopt these 10 traits as a lifestyle, they can actually free us to live in security and strength.

Need an example? Take James. If only he would have stayed within one of the clear fences set down in Psalm 15: "He . . . speaks truth in his heart."

James just happened to be walking by the fax machine at his sales office one day when a fax rumbled in. No one was around when he picked up the page and read it. And no one saw him go quickly to the copy machine and make his own copy before replacing the original in the machine.

The paper he held contained a red-hot lead on a lucrative piece of real estate that had just come on the market—and it was addressed to another agent in the office. But armed with his inside information, James called one of his own clients and in no time had beat his unsuspecting office partner to the prize.

Shrewd business tactics? Just another example of the "you snooze, you lose" principle? No. It was flat-out thievery. And although James had been sure no one had seen him remove the fax from the machine, he didn't know that someone had watched him put it back.

When confronted about it later, he lied. That's when they "froze" the files in his office, and a careful search turned up the copy he'd made of the fax. That find led to his dismissal, a major lawsuit, and disgrace.

Speaking the truth. Isn't that awfully restrictive? Not at all. Like each element in the list of 10 in Psalm 15, it's full of freedom and life. What's more, practicing all 10 can virtually eliminate our Maalox bills and offers a better guarantee than Sominex for bringing on a good night's sleep.

"Halt! Who Goes There?"

Have you ever been asked a question that really wasn't a question? Like when your mother caught you with chocolate all over your mouth and hands and asked, "Have you been into those cookies?"

Or the policeman who stops you when you're racing to an appointment and says, "Did you know you were speeding?"

Those are called rhetorical questions because we already know the answers—they're obvious! Psalm 15 starts with two of those questions: "O Lord, who may abide in Thy tent? Who may dwell on Thy holy hill?"

David knew the answer, and he told us in detail in the verses that follow. But he did much more than just pick the Jeopardy category "Things I Already Know" for $50. Like a sentry guarding a gate, these two opening questions form a password that travelers who want to come and worship God need to know.

Throughout the ancient world, there was a pattern of question and answer that commonly met a person desiring entrance into a place of worship. For example, one inscription on an Egyptian temple warned all who dared enter, "He who comes here must be pure. Therefore, purify yourself fittingly at the entrance of the great god's temple." So, David's use of the twin questions that start this psalm is almost like a sentry challenging a figure he sees in the night.

That's an unusual element of this psalm. In fact, out of all 150 psalms, only two are classified as "entrance" psalms.

Throughout history, knowing and asking for a password was a major thing. During the Civil War, for example, the South suffered a crippling loss when a password wasn't used. A sentry from the Eighteenth North Carolina Regiment failed to call out, "Halt! Who goes there?" at a place named Chancellorsville. Instead, on a dark night, he picked up his musket and fired at a cluster of men riding toward him—mortally wounding his own General Stonewall Jackson. In many ways, the South never recovered from losing Jackson's leadership. In fact, his commanding officer, Robert E. Lee, said, "His passing leaves a hole we cannot replace."

"Halt! Who goes there?"

David didn't leave out this challenge to those who would worship God. He asked clearly and boldly two questions that await—that demand—a response. And David gave us the answers to both in this psalm.

An Internal Aerobics Program

Do you detest exercise videos as much as we do? I (Rick) am a jogger, and I (John) regularly risk my life on my mountain bike. It's not the exercise we resent. It's how those exercise videos often come packaged with a hyperactive aerobics instructor and five "totally fit" friends alongside who never seem to sweat.

Yet, we agree that there's one instructor whose class we'd sign up for— King David—because we would certainly receive a full-body workout when it comes to our faith. Just look at the "active" words used throughout the psalm:

Abide . . . dwell . . . walk . . . work . . . speak . . . as well as some of the major body parts that get mentioned: heart . . . tongue . . . eye.

No spectators here. It's time to get down to the hard work of anchoring our lives in godly character. In a sweaty, push-yourself-to-the-limit physical workout, you actually stretch and make minor tears in the muscle fibers. But as those fibers grow back together, they become stronger than they were before. Likewise spiritually, as we begin to use these muscles of godly character—as we stretch and strain to put them into practice—we will be strengthening them, making them a useful part of our lives, and exercising our faith into a state of spiritual fitness.

The Curtain's Going Up

You now know who wrote Psalm 15, why he listed 10 qualities that compose an unshakable lifestyle, and how the two questions he posed at the beginning of the psalm form a unique password to those who would worship in God's presence. The previews are over, and we're ready to look at the main feature frame by frame. As we turn to the first verse of Psalm 15, get ready for an active experience in strengthening each aspect of your faith. From top to bottom, this is a psalm that was made to be applied. And our journey begins by facing the most important questions we'll ever answer.

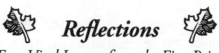 ***Reflections***

Four Vital Lessons from the Fine Print

1. Does it surprise you that a great saint like David had so many human weaknesses? Why or why not?

2. As John and Rick pointed out, David went through many extremes during his lifetime. What highs and lows have you gone through in yours?

3. John and Rick mention that David had a center to his life that never changed. Without reading ahead, what or where do you believe that center was?

4. What would you consider to be the center of your life? What kind of strength or stability does it give you? Are you satisfied with that amount? Why or why not?

5. John and Rick state that God likes lists. Why not pick one of those mentioned in this chapter (Prov. 6:16–19; Gal. 5:22–23; 2 Pet. 1:5–8; Rev. 2:1–3:22) and study it? Perhaps you could memorize it as well.

6. How do you feel when you are inside a fence? Do you feel safe and secure or resentful? Why? In your everyday actions, do you stay within the boundaries or explore ways of getting around them? Why do you think you respond that way?

7. Reread the story of James and the fax machine. Have you ever been tempted to do something unethical at work or school? What did you do, and how did you feel afterward?

Chapter 5

The Two Most Important Questions You'll Ever Answer

O Lord, who may abide in Thy tent?

What could make conservative businessmen, protective parents, and even physically challenged men and women cross a sun-baked wilderness, complete with wild animals and bandits? For many, it was a once-in-a-lifetime opportunity. From all parts of the kingdom, they came by donkey, camel, or foot. And as they made the difficult climb toward the great temple (found in a place called the City on the Hill), they saw a mountain in the distance.

"Mount Moriah!" they cried. "Beyond it . . . Jerusalem!"

So went the story of literally thousands of weary pilgrims during the golden days of Israel's history. Like Muslims today making pilgrimages to Mecca, going to Jerusalem for Passover was a Jew's dream come true. And just as the pioneers in our own country made up songs as they moved west, so, too, did the pilgrims of David's day sing, especially psalms, to help melt away the miles as they traveled to the Holy City.

Many biblical scholars look at Psalm 15 as a 1000 B.C. version of "Onward, Christian Soldiers." It was a song that roused weary pilgrims to lighten their steps and swing their arms as they made their long-dreamed-of trek to Jerusalem.

David's words, which were also sung in worship inside the tabernacle, began with a question—actually, two questions. In fact, they're the most challenging and potentially life-changing questions we'll ever have to answer.

The Starting Place for an Unshakable Life

In this chapter, we'll look at the first question David asked: "O Lord, who may abide in Thy tent?" Put in the Trent-Hicks translation: "O Lord, who may be Your traveling companion on earth?"

What's so special about these opening words? They speak of a deep need each of us has as we travel through life. It's a need I (John) saw as a young boy.

Starfish Memories

If I squint my eyes and take a long look back in my memory, I can see miles of bright, sunny beaches. Waves splash on jagged rocks, creating small pools that contain enough sea life to keep three young boys occupied for hours.

I grew up in a single-parent home with a wise, caring, overworked mother. But her workload didn't stop her from calling us boys outside one afternoon to see what had "followed" her home. It was a tiny aluminum trailer called a teardrop because of its unique shape. It was obviously well used and couldn't have been over seven feet long. When you opened the single side door, there was a full-size mattress inside—just big enough for the four of us huddled in our sleeping bags. And though it wasn't tall enough for even us boys to stand inside, there was still room to cram in all the "essentials" we needed on a camping trip—things like sodas, armies of toy soldiers, mountains of snacks, softball gloves, footballs, and swimsuits.

My mother had grown up in affluence and had never been camping as a child. Yet, with three active boys ages five, five, and seven (me, my twin brother, Jeff, and my older brother, Joe), she felt strongly that we needed some "outdoor education." It was 1957, long before any organized single-parent support groups. So, all alone, she bravely loaded up the trailer and us boys for a six-hour trek through the desert from Phoenix down to the Mexican border. From there, it was another three hours to a place the gringos called Rocky Point, the Mexicans called Punta Penasco, and we boys came to call Kid Heaven.

But not that first night.

Mom had never used a Coleman heater, lantern, or stove, so after hours of us taking turns trying to get anything lit, we ate a cereal dinner by weakening flashlight. When we woke up, a cold wind was pounding the trailer and sand-blasting our faces when we peeked outside.

Huddled together, we were just about ready to toss in the towel and head home when a caravan of trucks and trailers drove into our campsite. Soon dads, moms, and kids of all ages were piling out, setting up tents, and even getting stoves lit for hot cocoa and coffee. We watched them enviously as they laughed and warmed themselves with a roaring campfire they quickly had going. And that's when something special happened.

I'm not sure what motivated him to do so, but after a while, a middle-aged man with a smiling, weather-beaten face walked over. The smile had stayed through raising three now-grown sons of his own. And the weather-beaten look came from being a deck officer on a destroyer during the Second World War.

He invited us to join the rest of them around the warmth of the fire, and when asked, he told us to call him "Uncle Don. Everybody else does."

What we had happened upon in the night was the favorite campsite of an unofficial "camping club" from Phoenix. They were a group of business-people who took off their ties, gathered their families, and came down to Rocky Point nearly every other weekend. And as it turned out, their unofficial leader was Uncle Don.

While my mother appreciated the coffee, the adult company, the safety of a group, and later the lessons in getting our stove and lantern in ship shape, three father-starved boys saw something else. We saw a man's man who actually liked kids and who took us under his wing that day . . . and for many weekends thereafter.

By Sunday noon, the weather had cleared, the sun was out, and we'd been up and down the beach a hundred times. The last thing we wanted was to pack up and leave. But leave we did after one more thing happened—our family was officially asked to join the Cholla Bay Wading and Burnt Food Society by Uncle Don himself.

I can't explain to you the incredible relief that came over us when the invitation came to "pitch our tent" with these veteran campers. (If you've been a novice camper, maybe you *can* imagine.) It meant we wouldn't be alone in a strange country where we didn't know the language. We had a guide to show us the ropes, friends to watch our gear when we were at the beach, and a warm fire to turn to if we couldn't get ours started.

In many ways, that's a reflection of the first question David asked in Psalm 15.

Come Inside My Tent

Put in the literal language of a shepherd who had camped out many nights himself, it reads: "O Lord, who may sojourn in Thy tent?"

A "sojourner" during David's time was someone passing through, not a permanent resident. As such, he was someone without the rights of a citizen, making him dependent on the hospitality of others to provide sustenance and point out the watering holes and places of safe passage.

Today, hospitality to strangers is about as rare as the IRS sending a thank-you note for filing your taxes on time (with an extra refund check tossed in). But in David's day, when hotels and road maps were next to nonexistent, hospitality was expected—*required*—and often a life-or-death necessity. In fact, if you weren't hospitable to travelers, it wasn't quickly forgotten.

From the Book of Deuteronomy, listen to Moses' stinging words of judgment to a group of people who refused hospitality to God's people: "No Ammonite or Moabite shall enter the assembly of the Lord; none of their descendants, even to the tenth generation, shall ever enter the assembly of the Lord" (Deut. 23:3).

At a minimum, that's two entire nations who were cut off from God's presence and place of worship for almost 400 years. Why so severe? Moses provided the answer in Deuteronomy 23:4: "Because they did not meet you with food and water on the way when you came out of Egypt" and because they attempted to curse God's people as well.

God's people suffered when they couldn't come inside the tents of the Ammonites and Moabites on their journey. They received no warmth from the cold, no water for parched lips or weary animals, no blessing to encourage their spirits.

In contrast, can you imagine the relief of traveling in a strange place with Someone as your guide who created the very ground you walk on? Or being able to sit and ask questions from the same Person who knows your future and can also bring peace and healing to your troubled past? The same One who invites you to drink from "quiet waters" and protects you as powerfully as a mighty eagle sheltering her young under her wings?

That's the invitation David raised in his question. Who is it that can share God's tent? Who gets to "camp out" with the King of kings and Lord of lords? Who has access to the most sacred of tents, called the tabernacle, where the Jews went to worship God?

In the rest of Psalm 15, David told us in detail just who the "who" is. In fact, we'll see that there are 10 specific aspects of "dwelling in His tent" reflected in the verses to come. But one thing is certain: As the old hymn says, "This world is not my home. / I'm just a-passing through." We're all sojourners when it comes to our few days on earth. We're all "strangers and aliens." We all long for a permanent home someday. We all need help from others. We're all looking for a place of refreshment, peace, and rest.

So stop and ask yourself, do you know for sure that you have a safe place tucked away in God's tent? You can know, just as you can know for certain the answer to David's next question—one that concerns an *eternal* camping spot.

Reflections

The Two Most Important Questions You'll Ever Answer

1. Think of a time when you felt alone and then someone came along and made you feel accepted and welcomed. What did the person do that helped you feel a part of the group or situation?

2. Like the old hymn "Just a Closer Walk with Thee," what causes you to feel God's closeness and care the most?

3. Step inside God's tent and take a better look at His closeness and character by reading Psalm 103.

Chapter 6

The Answer That Leads You Home

Who may dwell on Thy holy hill?

There's nothing like returning home after a long trip—to your street, your yard (with grass that desperately needs mowing), your own bed (instead of Aunt Harriet's daybed—called that because it doesn't allow you to sleep at night), and, best of all, your own pillow (instead of those rock-hard neck killers).

It's the same feeling you get when five of you have been bottled up in a tiny apartment and then you get the chance to move into a three-bedroom house complete with a big yard. No more listening to elephants being herded in the apartment above you or rock music blaring at 1:00 A.M. from the apartment next door.

Now you've got your own place where you can stretch out, where you can plant a sapling that will grow into a towering tree, where you can wake to the sounds of birds and crickets instead of woofers and tweeters.

That same relief in coming home is what David pictured in the second question he asked in Psalm 15: "Who may dwell on Thy holy hill?"

David had already hinted that he knew who could "pitch his tent" with Almighty God. Now he asked, "Which sojourner can stop and unpack, end his or her travels, and move in for good?"

Making Long-Term Reservations at a Heavenly Home

To quote one biblical scholar, "[To dwell] stresses the idea of a longer or permanent stay, rather than just an overnight hop. The Hebrew word here underscores the idea of nearness, closeness, and permanence."[1] It's a word that literally means to "settle down; to remain; especially at peace, rest, and security."

Isn't that what we all want?

All of us long for a place of peace and security that we can call home. Maybe lakefront property or someplace with mountain views. But a holy hill?

In Scripture, God's holy hill was far better than any beachfront property or gated community. It was always a reference to Mount Zion, that holiest of places where God's presence actually dwelled with His people in bodily form. It was there that Jerusalem was built, the Ark of the Covenant was taken, and later, where the magnificent temple of Solomon was constructed.

Mount Zion became much more than just a mound of dirt and rocks. It became a symbol for the best place we could ever be—in God's presence. That was why one devoted pilgrim wrote in Psalm 84 (v. 10),

> For a day in Thy courts is better than a thousand outside.
> I would rather stand at the threshold of the house of my God, than dwell in the tents of wickedness.

Mount Zion was the "city of the Great King," and in the Book of Revelation, it becomes the site of the "heavenly Jerusalem," where God will dwell with humanity forever. "Blessed are those who wash their robes, that they may . . . enter by the gates into the city!" (Rev. 22:14).

Both questions that David asked at the beginning of Psalm 15 apply to the same person. The same man or woman who is able to sojourn with God day by day is the one who can move in and dwell with Him in heaven forever. But who is that person? More important, is there a way you can know for certain that that person is you?

An Opportunity to Answer the Question of a Lifetime

We know that questions can make people uncomfortable. For example, we all remember the scary experience of being called on in class. It's amazing how much short-term memory loss can occur when a teacher asks a simple question. Whether we were prepared or not, for most of us, the mere fact of the teacher looking in our direction for a "volunteer" caused blood pressure to go up, palms to sweat, and voices to rise two octaves.

At the beginning of this psalm, David asked two questions we dare not ignore. No pretending to drop a piece of paper and ducking out of sight. No passing off the answer to a best friend or spouse.

The plain fact is, each of us has the chance, right now, to answer David's questions. Each of us has the opportunity, for now and forever, to enter into a personal relationship with Almighty God—to move from a passing stranger to a prized son or daughter of a heavenly Father who offers His tent to shelter us on earth and who provides His holy hill for us to dwell on for eternity.

But how do we answer David's questions? What words can we use? What actions are required?

We each have a unique life story that God uses to reveal Himself to us. But all roads end at the same place—a rugged hill and a blood-stained cross, where a willing Savior gave His life-blood for us. God desires that each of us would say yes to David's questions—that we would tell Him, "Lord, I can walk with You day by day. And because of what You've done for me, I've got a place with You in heaven." But it takes a response on our part. A committing of our lives. Confessing our sin. Surrendering to His love.

Don't think that by putting this book down now you can escape these questions or God's gentle calling. As C.S. Lewis pointed out, none of us is safe from God's love. In the most unlikely ways and places, His love seeks us out and gently nudges us toward a personal relationship with Him.

Just as He did for me (Rick). Patiently. Unexpectedly. Persistently. God never stopped revealing Himself to me. Even when I wasn't listening; even when I was convinced I didn't need Him; even when I ridiculed those who told me about Him.

How I came to know Christ is a testimony that He can reach anyone, anywhere, anytime.

Purple Haze to a Pliable Heart

I was raised in Southern California by parents who were supportive but not Christians. In fact, the only Christian influence I had as a child came from spending my summers in Kentucky, working on my great-grandparents' farm.

This was a completely different environment for me. The weeks were filled with doing chores, riding horses, and going fishing, but Sundays were set aside for something new. Every week, my great-grandmother, who was a committed Christian, would take my older brother, Rod, and me to church.

He Whispered to Me as a Child

One Sunday, the pastor asked anyone who wanted to invite Christ into his or her life to come forward. I was busy drawing on an offering envelope and not paying attention, but the next thing I knew, Rod had slipped out of the pew and was walking forward.

I always looked up to my big brother, so I thought, *If he's going up there, I should, too.* But I took one step down that aisle, thought *Naaaah!* and sat down.

The next morning when I woke up, I heard my brother in bed singing, "I took Jesus as my Savior; you take Him, too," and I thought maybe I should take Jesus as my Savior. But when I quizzed my great-grandmother about it, she asked me two pointed questions that postponed my making that decision for another 10 years: "Do you know what it means to ask Jesus into your life? And are you ready to do it?"

Well, I didn't understand what it was about, and without further explanation, I chose not to do it then.

He Nudged Me in My Teens

Years went by, and the next time I was confronted with my need for Christ was in high school. At that time, I lived for sports and was doing well on the football team. But my sophomore year, on the last day of the last week of the season, my coach saw me smoking as I was walking to school.

Coach called me into his office and kicked me off the team. I lost my letter and the chance to play in the last game of the season. I was devastated. Just moments after that happened, I went to my locker, intending to take my jersey as a "souvenir," and I found that they'd cleaned it out. Nothing was left but my cleats and a pair of dirty socks I hadn't washed all season—still standing up by themselves!

This was the first time that something I had lived for had let me down. It was the first time I felt inadequate and really depressed. It wouldn't be the last.

During my remaining years in high school, I did what was typical for a lot of teenagers in Southern California in the sixties. I became a hippie, complete with long hair, alcohol, and drugs. At the time, I was really enjoying myself and was content with my freewheeling lifestyle. Then came Easter break during my senior year.

He Called Me at a River

In my circle of friends, you really had only two choices over spring break—go to Balboa Island or to the Colorado River. A friend and I decided to go to the river, and we started making plans. We both owned VWs, but neither one was good enough to endure that kind of journey. So we took the most reliable parts of the two cars, combined them into one mostly adequate car, and started on our trip.

We headed down the road, and after about an hour, I asked my friend, "So, where is the river?"

"I thought you knew!" he said.

Since neither of us knew where we were going, we pulled off the freeway and had a mechanic at a gas station draw us a map, on a Jack-in-the-Box napkin, to Parker, Arizona.

It took us twice as long to get there as it should have due to breakdowns and getting lost, but we finally arrived just before sunup. We tried to sleep in the back of the VW, but when the sun rose, it was like trying to sleep in a microwave oven.

We got up and decided some breakfast might help us feel better. We went to a restaurant, but the food was bad. Our moods got worse, and less than an hour into our vacation, we decided to head home.

Actually, though our intent was to go home to L.A., we accidentally started driving in the opposite direction, toward Phoenix. Then something amazing happened. As we were driving, we suddenly saw my best friend from California, Russ Hicks (no relation), standing on the side of the road.

He recognized my car (it had some psychedelic flowers painted on the sides that made it hard to miss) and waved us over. I hadn't even known he was going to be there. He told us that some of our friends were camping at the Blue Water Marina, and he invited us to stay with them. We hopped the fence to avoid the camping fee and joined the group.

Shortly after we arrived, because I looked older than anyone else in the group, my friends gave me their money to buy beer. I came back with plenty of beer, but it turned out that they had given me *all* their money. Now we had no gas money for our almost-empty cars and no food for an entire week at the river. But we had plenty to drink, and to our warped sense of logic, a liquid diet was just fine.

Divine Appointments

As we set out to drink away our holiday, we soon had company. Who should end up next to us but a youth group from a church near where we lived in Southern California! Before long, some of the girls from the group came by and asked, "Have you ever heard of the Four Spiritual Laws?"

After we heckled them a bit, they brought over their young youth pastor, Kent Hughes, who found out we didn't have any food. As part of their outreach plan, they had brought twice as much food as they needed, so they invited us to eat with them. We were reluctant because we assumed they would preach to us over the meals, but they promised not to talk about God unless we asked them.

Finally, the hunger pangs won out over our arrogance, and we graciously allowed them to feed us. As we hung out with these people, I saw for the first time how Christianity should be lived out. We ended up letting them share their faith with us, and at the end of the week, Kent confronted us with the claims of Jesus Christ and asked if we wanted to become Christians.

My first thought was, *I don't want to die and go to hell, because hell is probably a lot like Parker, Arizona.* On the other hand, I didn't want to live the lifestyle of those geeky teenagers I'd seen all week. At the time, I was too cool for that, so I declined the offer again. But my best friend, Russ, decided then and there to turn his life over to Christ.

Before we left, Kent did one more thing. He filled our gas tanks. We drove back to Long Beach and made it to within one house of my friend's home before we ran out of gas!

My brother . . . my best friend . . . both had turned to Christ. But not me. Not yet.

Falling from on Top of the World

Because of my lifestyle and some bad choices I'd made, I ended up finishing high school at a continuation school. I was kicked out of junior college, and that left me plenty of time to hang around at the beach for about a year.

One day, my girlfriend's father took pity on me. I guess he saw potential in me, because he offered me a significant position in his Hollywood business. Overnight I went from a beach bum to a junior-grade executive, complete with a profit-sharing plan, company car, and new suit.

It was a successful, gratifying year of having all my needs met. Once again I thought I was on top of the world . . . and once again I realized it wasn't enough.

One day on the freeway, while driving home from work, I had what seemed at the time to be a vision from God (or an LSD flashback). I saw a line of cars backed up on the freeway for miles. It reminded me of a line of ants dutifully marching into their anthill at night. The next morning they would march out again.

What a trap! There just had to be more to life than that.

Then it hit me. I remembered what those people at the river had told me about the sin in my life separating me from God. Maybe God could bring more meaning into my life. They had said that God loves me. That He sent His Son, Jesus, to die on the cross to pay the penalty for my sins so that I could have a relationship with God and have eternal life. All I had to do was believe it, confess how I'd fallen short, and ask Jesus Christ to come in and take charge of my life.

That day I went home, opened my Bible, and asked Jesus into my life. Though I can't explain it all, at that moment I knew that the God of the universe was in my life. From then on, changes began to naturally take place in me.

I started eliminating activities that didn't fit the new life God had given me. I had a real desire to share what I had learned and experienced about God. I even spent time hitchhiking around the country with a friend, and we discussed Christ with everyone who picked us up.

Eventually, I ended up going to Kent Hughes's church. There something else happened. I started dating a girl I'd met once before, a young lady who had been a part of that same youth group that camped next to us on the Colorado River. And as evidence of how much God had changed me (we were definitely not attracted to each other at the river), that girl became my wife. We've since enjoyed more than 21 great years of marriage, living the Christian life together.

It's Your Turn

Perhaps no one has ever directly asked you to accept Jesus Christ as your Lord and Savior. Maybe you've felt Him tugging at your sleeve, but you've never stopped and faced Him.

It's your turn now.

Before we look any further at this wonderful, powerful psalm, you can't afford to skip over its opening questions. That's because one day when this life is over, each of us will stand and have to give an answer. And the only one that will open the door to life with Christ both now and in eternity is that we placed our faith in Him while we were on earth.

If you're already a Christian, this would be a great time to put down this book and take a few minutes to thank God for all He's done for you. And if you're ready to take that step and become a follower of Christ, you can acknowledge that fact by reading aloud a simple prayer. It's not a formula—just a suggestion for how you might want to begin this wonderful, life-changing adventure called the Christian life.

Dear Lord, I thank You for loving me all the days of my life. For calling me when I didn't hear You. For saving me when I didn't know I needed a Savior. I now know that Christ died for my sins and was resurrected so that I might live with joy, both here on earth and eternally with You in heaven. I humbly turn my life over to You and ask You to forgive my sins and cleanse my whole heart and life. I ask You to take control of my present and future and teach me to walk next to You each day.

That's the kind of prayer I (John) prayed as a high-school student with my Young Life leader, Doug Barram, next to me. Perhaps you're all by yourself now, and you've just prayed this prayer. If so, then pick up the phone, wake up your spouse, or walk over to a loved one or supportive neighbor and describe what you've done. You've not only accepted the greatest invitation you'll ever be offered, but you've just answered David's two questions as well.

O Lord, who may abide in Thy tent?

_____

(Write in your name and the date here.)

Who may dwell on Thy holy hill?

_____

(Write in your name and the date here.)

If you've just filled in these blanks for the first time, welcome to the family! You may not have heard any whistles or bells when you signed your name, but if you were in heaven right now, you would certainly hear angels rejoicing. (Look up Luke 15:7 in a Bible soon.) We rejoice with you as well.

We'd also like to do something else. We'd like to send you a booklet that can help you in your first steps as a Christian. Just write us with your story and include your return address. We'll send you this short guide to important things like getting into God's Word, praying to your heavenly Father, and finding a supportive church where you can begin to fellowship with your new family.

Meanwhile, if you're wondering what to do now that you're a Christian, you couldn't have picked a better road map to follow than the one traced out in Psalm 15.

As we close our look at these first two questions that concern our ultimate destiny, we'd urge you to commit to memory the words of a great verse that promises a present reality. It's found in 2 Corinthians 5:17: "If any man is in Christ, he is a new creature; the old things passed away; behold, new things have come."

With that new creation comes the cornerstone to an unshakable life—a personal relationship with Jesus Christ. And to get a guided tour of what a rock-solid Christian life looks like—your new life—study the 10 traits that follow in Psalm 15. But first, on the following few pages, we've provided the Trent-Hicks Stability Inventory to help you gauge the present condition of your life with regard to these 10 traits. Just how solid are your faith and character today? What areas do you most need to work at developing? This simple self-test will give you some answers.

We'd love to hear from you if you've trusted Christ as your Savior. Contact John Trent and Rick Hicks at Encouraging Words, 12629 N. Tatum Blvd., Phoenix, AZ 85032.

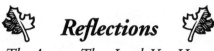 **Reflections**

The Answer That Leads You Home

1. John and Rick state that we all long for a place of peace and security that we can call home. Take time to evaluate your security level in the following areas:

   The level of security I felt as a child in my home was . . .

   Very Insecure   *Very Secure*
   1   2   3   4   5   6   7   8   9   10

   The level of security I feel in my church home is . . .

   Very Insecure   *Very Secure*
   1   2   3   4   5   6   7   8   9   10

   The level of peace I feel in my relationship with Christ is . . .

   Anxious   *Peacefully secure*
   1   2   3   4   5   6   7   8   9   10

2. This chapter asks a pointed question: "Have you asked Jesus Christ into your life as your Lord and Savior?" If you have, give a brief description of your testimony. If you haven't, list the major hindrances that are stopping you from making this most important decision.

3. If you're still on the fence when it comes to committing your life to Christ, we urge you to read about two other people who had serious doubts themselves, yet found the new life God offers. See John 3:1–21 and Acts 9:1–19.

A Personal Evaluation Point

The Trent-Hicks Stability Inventory

Character Tune-up

Isn't it amazing how much cars have changed over the past few years? There are so many new advancements, and many of those high-tech inventions actually help. If you're having a problem with your car, you can take it to a mechanic who can plug it into a computer, and in a moment's time, you'll get an accurate diagnosis of the situation. You can even detect a problem before it becomes serious. The computer can identify things that otherwise can't be seen.

Wouldn't it be great if we could do the same with our lives—if we could just plug ourselves in and get a complete computer diagnostic print-out of what is wrong in our hearts . . . what "level" our spiritual lives are on . . . what areas in our characters need a "5,000-Day Checkup"?

Well, we can't give computer printouts or written guarantees. But we can give you a "diagnostic instrument" that can provide an idea of where you are in developing a rock-solid character.

Take a few minutes to look under the hood of your life, and see if you're running smoothly or need a tune-up. Then in about six months, redo the process and chart the progress you've made. You'll see how the 10 keys in Psalm 15 have positively affected your life.

How to Take This Inventory

Read each question through completely and thoughtfully. It helps if you can relate it to a real-life situation. Then circle the number that best represents how you would actually respond in that situation. Remember to answer honestly, as you really are today, not with what you think is right or how you would like to be.

Part I
Anchoring Our Personal Lives Index

Answer the following questions on a 1 to 7 scale.

1. When you talk to people, are your comments sincere, or do you sometimes put on a front, speaking in such a way as to create a misleading impression?

   Struggle with sincerity   *Always sincere*
   1   2   3   4   5   6   7

2. You've just received a second reimbursement check for the same business trip. You know your company's bookkeeping process, and there's no way they can trace this back to you once you cash it. How difficult would it be for you to not cash the check?

   Real difficulty in not cashing it   *Absolutely wouldn't*
   1   2   3   4   5   6   7

3. When someone does something that really offends you, how difficult is it for you to forgive the person?

   Difficult to forgive   *Desire to forgive*
   1   2   3   4   5   6   7

4. The programs I watch on television . . .

   Frequently watch violent/suggestive shows   *G-rated TV habits*
   1   2   3   4   5   6   7

5. Do you make a habit of doing "first things first," or do "urgent" but relatively unimportant things fill your day?

   Urgency dictates my day   *Focused on what's important*
   | 1 | 2 | 3 | 4 | 5 | 6 | 7 |

6. Is it difficult for you to accept that faith alone is what qualifies you for God's presence?

   Feel I need to earn my relationship with God   *Life based on faith alone*
   | 1 | 2 | 3 | 4 | 5 | 6 | 7 |

7. By honest evaluation, do you use "white lies" at work?

   Struggle with "white lies"   *Always speak truthfully*
   | 1 | 2 | 3 | 4 | 5 | 6 | 7 |

8. When you hit times of trial, do you typically tell yourself, "I'm still valuable in God's eyes" or "Perhaps God is punishing me or isn't with me."

   Struggle feeling acceptable to God   *Never question His acceptance*
   | 1 | 2 | 3 | 4 | 5 | 6 | 7 |

Part II
Protecting Our Most Important Relationships Index

9. If you're frustrated by someone, how likely are you to exaggerate a story to put the person in a bad light?

   I do this often   *I wouldn't do it*
   | 1 | 2 | 3 | 4 | 5 | 6 | 7 |

10. If you're offended by, wronged by, or dislike someone, do you find yourself looking for opportunities to discredit the person?

    Never   *Always*
    | 1 | 2 | 3 | 4 | 5 | 6 | 7 |

11. When put in a situation where seeking your desires infringes on someone else's well-being, how much do you consider the negative effect it will have on the other person?

    I have my rights; others' well-being is not my concern.   *The well-being of others is an important consideration for me.*
    | 1 | 2 | 3 | 4 | 5 | 6 | 7 |

12. There's a person who has a history of making life difficult for you. You're now in a situation that would give you a chance to get even. How likely is it that you'll take advantage of this opportunity?

I'll do it in a heartbeat!			*In spite of everything, I won't hurt someone else.*			
1	2	3	4	5	6	7

13. At work, if you heard something negative about a co-worker, would you be likely to believe it right away or reserve judgment until you could investigate further and discern the truth?

Believe the worst				*Give the benefit of the doubt*		
1	2	3	4	5	6	7

14. Are you likely to abandon or remain loyal to a friend who has failed or is wrong in some situation?

Abandon					*Remain loyal*	
1	2	3	4	5	6	7

Part III
Guiding Our Public Walk Index

15. Are you inclined to make fun of other Christians whose beliefs, worship styles, or personalities are different from your own?

Inclined to make fun a lot				*Not inclined to make fun*		
1	2	3	4	5	6	7

16. Whom do you find yourself more impressed and influenced by?

Society's celebrities				*Individuals with godly character*		
1	2	3	4	5	6	7

17. You've made a commitment to someone, and later you get a better offer. What's your response?

Do what's best for me					*Keep my promise*	
1	2	3	4	5	6	7

18. How confident are your family and friends that you will fulfill your promises to them?

They believe it when they see it.				*They know my word is my bond.*		
1	2	3	4	5	6	7

19. You book a flight for a business trip with an airline that uses your personal frequent flyer miles. Your company will reimburse you for the airfare. You could have saved your company money by booking a cheaper flight on a different airline. In a situation like this, how likely would you be to charge your company only for the lowest price you could have booked?

Very unlikely   *A sure thing*

   1   2   3   4   5   6   7

20. You have a chance to take advantage of a profitable financial opportunity. You're also aware that going through with it will cause difficulties for several other people. How much do the ramifications for others influence your decision?

I don't give them much thought.   *They greatly influence my decision.*

   1   2   3   4   5   6   7

SCORING

Total all the numbers you circled = _____
Mark your total score with an "X" on the line below.

Turbulent Lifestyle   *Stable Lifestyle*

20   40   60   80   100   120   140

_____

Date _____

APPLICATION PROJECT

We encourage you to date your score above. Six months later, retake the inventory, and mark your second score below. Then compare the two scores to see if you've grown toward a more stable lifestyle.

Turbulent Lifestyle   *Stable Lifestyle*

20   40   60   80   100   120   140

_____

Date _____

At the end of six months, do you think your score will go up? Does it need to? Do you want it to? It won't go up by itself, but the concepts we present in the remaining pages of this book can help to give you:

- direction if you need it
- motivation if you want it
- a plan if you really desire to do it

If you're serious about building godly character, making the very ground you walk on feel more solid because you can withstand more of the unexpected turbulence of life, read on!

In the next few chapters, we'll describe 10 keys to an unshakable lifestyle. They're not just 10 good ideas, 10 clever ways to give you more personal confidence, or even 10 great suggestions. Found in Psalm 15, they carry God's promise that under their influence, we will never be shaken.

Part II

Ten Keys to an Unshakable Lifestyle

They Anchor Our Personal Life

Chapter 7

THE FIRST KEY

Walking with Integrity

He who walks with integrity . . .

olid ground.
It's something God promises we can all find.
It's *somewhere* God leads us in Psalm 15.
Like a road map guiding us away from fear and uncertainty and toward confidence and inner security, this psalm presents 10 lifestyle traits that affect each one of us. They're like 10 checkpoints on the path to godly character. As we see each one growing in our lives, we are reassured that we're going the right way, and we can feel the ground growing more firm under our feet. These traits fall into three clear sections:

- Three keys to anchoring our personal lives (v. 2)
- Three keys to building trust while avoiding damage to our most important relationships (v. 3)
- Four keys to walking wisely and securely in a shaken world (v. 4)

Three Keys to Anchoring Our Personal Lives

In Psalm 15, David began by focusing on the inside. He soon high-lighted specific behaviors to adopt or avoid, but he began by looking beneath our actions to the core of our wills, emotions, and decisions—to our hearts.

In pulling back the curtain on who we need to be inside, David wrote: "He who walks with integrity, and works righteousness, and speaks truth in his heart . . . "

How important are these three characteristics? Have you ever helped build a house or walked past one under construction? If so, you've no doubt seen the wooden form and stakes set up to pour the foundation. If you looked closer, you'd notice some things laid inside that form that run its entire length. They're long, steel rods called *rebars* that reinforce and pull the whole foundation together once the concrete is poured. And if local codes or trying soil conditions require it, the builder will crisscross the rebars, making the footing even more solid.

As we continue our look at Psalm 15, we'll see that integrity is like a long, steel rod that runs the length and breadth of a foundation. The additional rebars of righteousness and truth are crucial, too, tied in and crisscrossing the foundation on which all the other principles will be poured.

But there's no doubt that David set a life of integrity as the first element in solid ground. Just what is integrity? What does it look like up close? Why is it so crucial to gain and so catastrophic to lose? How can we make it more a part of our lives and, in turn, pass it down to future generations?

In the pages that follow, we'll answer these questions and illustrate, define, and instruct you on how this internal rebar can reinforce your own life. One more thing: If it has been a little while since your inner character visited the building supply store, you're in for some sticker shock. In our shaken world where compromise stacks the shelves and stout hearts are scarce, integrity comes at a high cost.

No Artificial Coloring

When Kathy and I (Rick) bought our first house as a young married couple, it was a real fixer-upper. While Kathy went to work on decorating the inside, one of the areas I focused on was the landscaping. That might have something to do with the fact that my father-in-law owns a nursery, and when he visits, I like my yard to look good.

It took a lot of work and a lot of time to spruce up the yard. But persistence paid off, and finally everything was looking good . . . except for one pesky problem I just couldn't solve. I couldn't get the grass to grow in the front parkway area around the gas meter. After a couple of months of trying everything to turn that brown spot green, I suddenly discovered what was wrong.

One day as I was working in the yard, I saw a repairman replacing the gas meter next door. Just to be social, I introduced myself and asked what had called him out. He said that because of the age of the houses in this tract, a number of the gas meters were failing and causing several types of problems.

"Oh!" I said as the light began to dawn. "I may be having a problem with my gas meter. Why don't you come and look at it?"

As soon as he walked over and saw that the grass wasn't growing around the meter, he said, "I know what your problem is. With these old meters . . ." He went on to explain that sometimes the part of the meter that registers how much gas is going through clogs up. That allows a bit of the gas to leak out, getting into the ground and contaminating the soil.

That seemed like a good explanation of my problem. At last I could get that taken care of and have a totally green lawn any father-in-law would be proud of.

But then the repairman said, "I'll bet your gas bill is really low, isn't it?"

"I pay about eight dollars per month," I said (which in 1978 wasn't all that low to us).

Then he explained that the average gas bill in our area was around $40 per month.

When I heard that, I knew that having green grass was going to cost me some serious greenbacks. So after we discussed this a little more, I asked if he could come over and replace my meter when he was through next door.

He paused a moment and then said with a twinkle in his eye, "There's no need to do that right now. If you keep it the way it is, you won't need to pay as much, and it won't do any more damage to the grass than it already has."

"Well, that sounds good," I said, "but if I'm not paying the right amount, it should be replaced so I can pay the proper amount to the gas company."

"Don't be stupid!" he almost shouted at me in disbelief. "Leave it the way it is and it'll be okay. Besides, nobody knows."

"But I know and you know," I said, "so we need to do something about it."

Like a tutor lecturing a thick-headed student, he tried again, "I'm telling you, if you won't tell anybody, there's no need for me to tell anyone."

Without wanting to insult him or put him on the spot, I said, "I know about it, and I don't want it on my conscience. So, why don't you go ahead and change the meter?"

At that point, the conversation ended abruptly. He refused to do the repair and said that if I wanted to get the meter changed, I'd have to call the gas company myself. They'd send someone else to take care of it.

I did go into the house and make the call, and a few days later, another repairman came out and did the work. And what did I get for my efforts? After they switched the meter, my bill actually rose to $45 per month.

As Kathy and I talked about what had happened, we realized that this was just round one in a fallen world's fight to push us toward compromise. Could we spare the extra $37 we now had to pay the gas company every month? No. It made our already tight budget even tighter. But right then and there, we committed ourselves, as a couple, to stand for integrity in all we'd do, no matter what the cost. That was over 15 years ago, and we've never regretted that decision.

We also learned a hard lesson about integrity. Namely, cutting corners may be cheap, but genuine integrity comes at a high cost.

We learned the hard lesson that cutting corners may be cheap, but genuine integrity comes at a high cost.

For anyone serious about a life of integrity, count on three things:

1. It's going to cost you money.
2. It often takes a great deal of time and effort.
3. It may not make you popular or respected by the world.

Let me (Rick) tell you another story that illustrates how these three facts can come into play in everyday life. When Kathy and I got our first credit card, we resolved to use it wisely and with integrity. Little did we know that our resolve would be tested the very first time we bought something with it.

We were shopping out of town one day, and I noticed some volleyball T-shirts on sale. Because I was the recreation director at Forest Home at that time, I figured the shirts would make great uniforms. When we went to pay for them, however, we realized we didn't have enough cash with us, so we pulled out our brand-new credit card.

As the next month passed, I waited eagerly for the bill to arrive so we could pay it off (we hadn't charged anything else) and begin establishing a good credit rating. But to my surprise, no bill came. We waited another month; still no bill. After the third month went by with no bill showing up in our mailbox, I called the store to see what had happened.

At first the clerk was confused about why I was calling. (What kind of nut would call to say he hadn't been charged for his purchase?) But he said he would take care of it.

Another month passed, and still no bill from the credit card company. I called the store again and repeated my lengthy explanation. Again I was assured the situation would be corrected. Well, it wasn't. And when I called the store a third time, I could hear the other clerks in the background, joking about my calls.

The manager finally told me to forget about it because the case was more trouble to him than it was worth. "Get a life!" he practically shouted, and then he hung up on me.

Living a life of integrity may not gain you the respect of those you're dealing with, like those clerks who thought I was some kind of nut making life inconvenient for them. It takes more time and effort to do the right thing, too, like taking the time to make multiple phone calls while trying to handle a situation honestly. And it may cost you extra money—those long-distance calls cost almost as much as the shirts!

Without question, the stakes are often much higher than $45 in gas bills or the price of a few shirts. John and I see the higher stakes in the lives of God's people. At times, it's a marriage, career, or entire reputation on the line. But the principle remains the same: God is asking us to do what is right, living a life of integrity in spite of the cost or inconvenience to us. That's the first thing to keep in mind as you seek to build a lifestyle that can never be shaken. Namely, the materials don't come at closeout prices, but the benefits of using them are more than worth the cost.

The Benefits of a Life of Integrity

We could list any number of advantages to laying down integrity at the deepest level of our lives, but we'd rather let God Himself do the talking. His Word points eloquently to the incredible promises and praise we gain from Him and our families when we adopt integrity as a lifestyle.

Integrity can move us up the ladder the right way: "I put in charge of Jerusalem my brother Hanani, along with Hananiah the commander of the citadel, because he was a man of integrity and feared God more than most men do" (Neh. 7:2, NIV). As we mentioned above, being a person of integrity often costs you points in the world's eyes. Yet in God's view, it's the quickest and clearest way to move toward His best, and wise people like Nehemiah always look for people of character to move up the ladder.

Integrity brings us clear guidance: "The integrity of the upright guides them, but the unfaithful are destroyed by their duplicity" (Prov. 11:3, NIV).

Integrity provides a nonslip surface for our feet: "The man of integrity walks securely, but he who takes crooked paths will be found out" (Prov. 10:9, NIV).

Integrity passes down a lasting inheritance: "The days of the blameless are known to the LORD, and their inheritance will endure forever" (Ps. 37:18, NIV).

Integrity gives an unfailing blessing to our children: "A righteous man who walks in his integrity—how blessed are his sons after him" (Prov. 20:7).

Integrity makes a poor person rich: "Better is a poor man who walks in his integrity than he who is perverse in speech and is a fool" (Prov. 19:1).

Integrity makes all people better: "For the LORD God is a sun and shield; the LORD gives grace and glory; no good thing does He withhold from those who walk uprightly" (Ps. 84:11).

Integrity passes the test of what pleases God: "I know, my God, that you test the heart and are pleased with integrity" (1 Chron. 29:17a, NIV).

Integrity makes us more like our Savior: " 'Teacher,' they said, 'we know you are a man of integrity' " (Matt. 22:16b, NIV).

Those are just a few of the benefits God says are ours when we set integrity under our feet. But what exactly is integrity? Good question. Let's give you a clear, biblical answer.

Without Cracks, Crevices, or Contamination

As it's used in the Bible, the word *integrity* carries the meaning of being "sound, complete, without blemish, crack, or defect." I (John) remember hearing a seminary professor describe one way the word was employed during biblical times. In that age without Corningware or Noritake china, people relied on clay dishes, cups, and pots. It took many hours for a potter to shape, fire (in a handmade kiln), and cool the piece he or she was making. Unfortunately, with the uneven heat of a wood-fired furnace, cracks would often show up in the clay during the cooling process.

For the true craftsman, that meant shattering the blemished piece and starting over. For the unscrupulous potter, it meant filling in the cracks with wax and painting over the whole thing. As you can imagine, the cracked vessel might hold up fine the first few times it was used. But especially if something hot was placed inside it, the wax would soon melt and expose the defect.

That's why honest potters began putting the inscription "Without Wax" on the bottom of their pots. It was an inscription that meant this was a vessel that had been skillfully made, had been through the fires, and had stood the test of time. It was a vessel of integrity.

When we say that godly people we respect (like Billy Graham, Dr. James Dobson, or a beloved pastor) are people of integrity, we mean they have been uniquely handcrafted by God with special strengths, they've been tested by the fires of trials, and they've stood the test of time. In short, each is a vessel of honor to God "without wax."

Integrity is an active word. Proverbs 11:3 tells us, "The integrity of the upright will guide them." The word describes an individual moving forward, confident in where he or she is going because of walking in the light of God's Word.

Are you a person of biblical integrity? Do you speak the truth no matter what people want to hear? Do you refuse to compromise when you're under stress? Do you honor commitments instead of opting for excuses? Do you stay as pure as you can in a sexually and materially polluted

world? When you die and people file into church for your memorial service, will they say of you, "He said what he meant and meant what he
said," or "You knew where she stood. You could trust her to do the right
thing"?

Most of all, will they say of you, "That's one person who didn't just
read God's Word but lived it"?

Does biblical integrity sound like too high a standard? Well, let's drop
our eyes from Scripture to *Webster's Dictionary* and see if its definition will
cut us any slack.

Doing a Word Search

To find out how the average person might define integrity, we can go
to the dictionary. *Webster's Dictionary* says *integrity* means "honesty," and
honesty is "trustworthiness and incorruptibility to a degree that one is
incapable of being false to a trust, a responsibility, or a pledge."

Are you incapable of being false to a trust to a loved one, a responsibility at home or work, or a pledge to a friend? Are you incapable of going
back on a commitment? When you give your word, do you keep it . . .
always?

We don't know about you, but we fail that stringent a test. We find
ourselves at times making promises and not being able to fulfill them. We
find we're capable of letting people down and even, reluctantly, going back
on our word. Sound like you, too? Perhaps we need Someone's help in
making this type of integrity a reality in our lives. Or perhaps it's just
these book definitions of integrity that are so convicting.

What about the *real* world? How would someone like a construction
worker define integrity?

Passing All the Codes

Actually, the concept of integrity is used frequently in the construction business. In this context, it's a technical term that refers to adherence
to building codes that ensure that the building being constructed will be
safe, even under stress. An engineer who does some work at Forest Home
gave me (Rick) this working description of structural integrity. He
explained that even if he were building something as simple as a wall, it
would need to be:

- properly designed
- in compliance with all building codes
- safe
- able to function as it was intended

Structural integrity is one of those things that isn't given much thought before it's tested. But toss in an earthquake or some South Dakota winds, and the lack of integrity can draw a great deal of attention.

As children, we learned a story that graphically illustrates the need for structural integrity. It's the timeless tale of "The Three Little Pigs." Now, in case your children are long past the bedtime-story stage (and even if they're not), let's briefly recap what happened. The three little pigs left home, and each built a house for himself. The houses were each made of different materials, with different degrees of structural integrity.

All three houses looked great . . . at first. But when the wolf came and challenged the pigs in the two rather hastily built homes, he huffed and puffed and blew down their houses.

The third little pig was wiser. His house took a little longer to erect since he followed the local "wolf-proofing" building codes. But he felt good about the structural integrity of his house when it was finally completed. Actually, his two brothers felt great about it because they had someplace to run when their houses crashed down. As the three of them stood behind those solid walls, the house endured all the huffing and puffing and did not blow down.

Remember the moral of the story? Houses (and lives) built without structural integrity won't stand up to the invasion of the enemy. Houses built with the right materials and workmanship will.

Scripture, *Webster's Dictionary,* and the construction world all paint a picture of integrity that seems lofty and unattainable—not at all something a child could grasp, right?

Think again.

A Child's View of Integrity

You need to learn to trust God for the daily strength to build biblical integrity into your life because, like it or not, your children will learn to define it first through your attitudes and actions.

Frank Gaebelein was founder of the Stony Brook School in New York and a co-founder of *Christianity Today*. But most of all, he was a man of utmost integrity. His daughter Gretchen wrote, "Long before I knew how to spell the word or even knew what it meant, I realized my father was a man of integrity. Later I would learn phrases like 'Christian commitment' and 'devotion to duty.' But from my earliest years, I simply knew that Frank Gaebelein 'rang true.'"

What a testimony! His life "rang true." If your children were asked to sum up your life, would they say that when the velvet hammer of success or the iron mallet of trials and failure struck your life, you rang true? We certainly hope that's the way our kids see us.

Whatever direction we turn from the word *integrity*, we're trapped. And that's how it should be. Our sinfulness and our need of God's saving grace should cause us to bow our heads before we look at the cross.

Lifting Our Eyes to the Source of Our Strength

Before you toss up your hands and write off a life of integrity as an exalted ideal that you'll never attain, look at one more picture. It's given in the Book of Numbers in the Old Testament, and it's a picture of a stubborn, hard-hearted people who were in deep trouble.

After Moses led God's people out of Egypt and into the wilderness, they griped and moaned and wished they were back in slavery. This angered God, who had miraculously provided for their deliverance, so He sent poisonous snakes among them. Any man, woman, or child who was bitten by these "horned serpents" quickly died. Yet, after the people repented and Moses petitioned God, He once again made a way of escape.

God had Moses make a bronze serpent and attach it to the cross beam of a tribal standard—like those that carried each of the 12 tribes' banners. Now the people had a choice. Whenever they were bitten by a snake, all they had to do was look at the snake on the cross and they were cured (see Num. 21:4-9).

One look at the right place and a person's death sentence was commuted. Can you see the New Testament parallel? Christ did. That's why He told a questioning Nicodemus one night, "As Moses lifted up the serpent in the wilderness, even so must the Son of Man be lifted up."

Never heard that verse? It comes just before John 3:16: "For God so loved the world, that He gave His only begotten Son, that whoever believes in Him should not perish, but have eternal life."

Jesus was telling Nicodemus there is only one place to look for everlasting life. And when we look at the right place, it makes all the difference.

How do you keep looking to Christ for the strength to maintain a life of integrity? Anne, a commodities broker, was greatly helped by a mirror that hung on the back of her office door in a large trading firm. In her job, she heard tidbits of news—inside information—every day that, if leaked to the right people, could make them (and her) a great deal of money.

Anne knew other brokers who had given in to the temptation and acted on such information, even though it was unethical and illegal. But whenever she felt the same enticement, she looked to the Lord for strength . . . and to that mirror on the back of her door. It appeared to be an ordinary rectangular mirror placed there so she could check her hair and her smile before she walked out of the office. But it also had these words taped across the bottom: "The woman who looks in this mirror has been bought with Jesus' shed blood. Make sure she lives like it."

That's the message Anne saw every time she looked up from her desk or spoke on the phone. It was a tangible reminder of her commitment to integrity in a working world where temptation abounded.

If you've been convicted about the level of integrity in your life, don't keep your head down. Look up to the One who took all our sins upon Himself on the cross. Ask His forgiveness for falling short on your commitments and convictions, and ask Him for the strength day by day—hour by hour, if necessary—to live a life of integrity. Perhaps a physical reminder like Anne's will help as well.

What you'll find in looking up to Christ is the power to live authentically, honestly, with integrity. What's more, you'll be able to link your practiced lifestyle of integrity with the added rebars of righteousness and truth, the next two keys to building a life that can never be shaken.

Reflections
Walking with Integrity

1. Reread the story about Rick and the gas meter. If you were in that situation, how would you have responded? (Be honest.)

2. Think of a time when your integrity was on the line. What was the situation, and how did it turn out? How did you feel about the outcome?

3. John and Rick list several benefits of integrity on page 60. Which of those is most valuable to you?

4. Read Psalm 16:8–11. List the descriptive words the psalmist used to paint a picture of stability in the life of the believer.

5. In your own words, how do you define *integrity?* Do you tend to view it more as a destination or as a journey?

6. Think of a person whom you consider to exemplify integrity. What actions in his or her life demonstrate this quality? How do you feel when you're in this person's presence?

7. Think of someone whom you consider to exemplify a *lack* of integrity. What actions in his or her life demonstrate the absence of this quality? How do you feel when you're in this individual's presence?

8. John and Rick told the story of Anne, the commodities broker who taped a helpful reminder to her office mirror. What reminder would be good for you to see every day? And where might you put it—on your bathroom mirror? refrigerator door? car dashboard? office desk?

Chapter 8

THE SECOND KEY

The Power to Choose What's Right

He who . . . works righteousness . . .

ome things just come naturally. Like the way a baby's eyes light up with her first taste of birthday cake and ice cream; the awe that sweeps over a first-time visitor when a beautiful sunset hits the multicolored rocks of the Grand Canyon; or the excitement (or fear) that hits everyone as their log noses over the 60-foot drop at Splash Mountain in Disneyland.

Other things take work. Like losing those last five pounds so that our weight is where it was when we *first* decided to go on a diet; devoting the 20 hours it takes to fill out the 10-page *simplified* 1040 form; or gathering the courage to ask that special person to the party of the year.

Still other things take work *and* prayer. Like golf!

If you're one of those people who sees a golf match on television and asks, "Why?" you really should get out on the course at least once in your life and tee off. I (Rick) am an avid golfer, and trust me—it's amazing how demanding a "recreational" sport can be.

Even one of golf's legends, Lee Trevino, acknowledged how challenging it is to hit that little white ball correctly. One day when a thunderstorm threatened to postpone a tournament he was playing in, he was asked if he was afraid he'd be hit by lightning since he was holding a metal club in his hand.

"Absolutely not!" Lee said, holding his club in the air. "Not even God can hit a one iron!"

Though we'd argue with Mr. Trevino's theology (and his view of God's accuracy), there's no argument that God's second key to an unshakable lifestyle comes complete with a far greater challenge. Those who want to build such a life must be ready to take on a full-time job. They'll get calluses on their hands and sweat on their brows as they daily "work righteousness."

What Is Righteousness? And Why Is It So Much Work?

Over 500 times in God's Word—139 times in the Book of Psalms alone—we run into the word *righteousness*. And though it may have been commonly understood in King James's time, its meaning has become obscure in our world of Prince Charles and Princess Di.

In the original language of the Old Testament, *righteousness* had several meanings. It meant "to be straight, to meet a standard, to be firm." In short, righteous action was behavior toward God and others that "toed the line," "kept on the straight and narrow," or "stayed within the boundaries."

I (John) learned an important and unexpected lesson that illustrates this definition at a seminar I did in beautiful, frigid Minnesota one February. At the end of a mild season, winter decided to show up on the particular weekend I was scheduled to do a conference there. It was 28 degrees below zero, with a bone-chilling, steady 25-mile-an-hour wind blowing—and that was during the daytime!

I'm from Phoenix, Arizona, home of dry heat, not blazing hearths. When traveling day came, I mowed my yard, packed my bags, raced to the airport, and hopped on the plane that would take me to the land of cold hands and warm hearts. After arriving at the airport, I picked up my rental car, pulled on my overcoat, gloves, and scarf, and dutifully read the instructions they handed me on what to do if my car wouldn't start in cold weather. Fortunately, my car did start, and I headed onto the freeway and to the conference site.

That's when I encountered near disaster.

I was in the far left lane of the freeway, heading directly into the sun, which had just peeked out from the clouds, when I noticed my windshield was getting awfully dirty. Muddy snow was being thrown up by cars in front of me, so I did what I always do in Arizona when I need a clearer perspective. I hit the "wash" button. Nothing like getting a lot of that soapy cleaning fluid all over your windshield to make it easy for the wipers to make things bright.

But I had failed to realize something veteran snow and ice drivers never forget. It was at least 40 degrees below zero (including the wind-chill factor), I was traveling 55 miles an hour on the freeway, and I had just made a *major* cold-weather driving mistake. Namely, you never hit the "wash" button in subzero weather.

It was so cold outside that the instant the cleaning liquid covered the windshield, it froze into a solid sheet of ice. Suddenly, I was totally blind in front and going full speed in the left lane of the freeway!

Life on a freeway becomes quite interesting when you can't see the traffic lanes anymore. I had never thought much about the benefits of "staying within the lines"—until now! Oh, how I wished I could have seen those white lines that stood for safety and direction!

It still amazes me that I was able to get off the road without harming myself or anyone else. Let's just say those next exciting moments on the freeway were the caffeine equivalent of drinking 20 Thirst-Buster-sized mugs of coffee. But I'd learned an indelible lesson about "staying between the lines" that day. If you want to avoid an automobile accident, you must be able to see and stay within prescribed boundaries.

The same thing is true with a righteous person. As part of staying within God's "tent" here on earth, he or she needs to see and stay within the lines when it comes to living before God and dealing with others.

But just like me hitting the "wash" button, there are times when we inadvertently (or more often purposely) blind ourselves to the white lines of God's Word and head right into trouble. In fact, God says one common characteristic of human beings is our inability to stay within the lines (see Rom. 3:23).

Why Is It So Hard to Live Righteously?

Inside all human beings, left over from Adam and perfected with each passing generation, is an instinctive drift toward sin. A pull toward compromise. A tug toward stretching the truth. A nudge toward envy, anger, pettiness, and greed. That includes us Christians. And it's something that will challenge us each day on this earth until we see the Lord face to face and are finally free of this fallen world.

It's like the story we heard of the college student who came back to her apartment and dropped a huge pile of books and papers on the kitchen table. "I've had it!" she said to her roommate. "I've got so much homework to do, I think I'm going to hire someone to take my final exam for me!"

"What course is it?" her roommate asked sympathetically.

"Ethics."

There's no doubt that in our cesspool society, we're being squeezed to cut corners and give in to compromise. But God is clear on His standards. In his readable translation of the New Testament, J. B. Phillips captured this tension between standing firm and selling out in Romans 12:2: "Don't let the world around you squeeze you into its own mould." But how often it does!

King David, in his psalm regarding the high cost of sin, wrote, "Behold, I was brought forth in iniquity, and in sin my mother conceived me"(Ps. 51:5). That's not saying there's anything sinful about the act of procreation or giving birth, but that even the newest baby comes complete with a propensity to wander off course. The apostle Paul reiterated this point in the Book of Romans, when he concluded that if he lined up all us "mature" folks, from the pastor to the person in the last pew, "There is none righteous, not even one" (Rom. 3:10).

But if that's true (and it is), we've got a major problem. Namely, we're *commanded* to be righteous. That's not only in Psalm 15 but throughout the Bible. The Lord Jesus Himself said that unless our righteousness is greater than that of the scribes and Pharisees, we'll never be able to enter the kingdom of God (see Matt. 5:20).

Talk about an impossible challenge!

The scribes and Pharisees were the same people who had hundreds of daily laws, rituals, and boundaries that they tried to keep themselves and force on others. And Jesus said our righteousness has to be better than theirs! From birth, we're incapable of being righteous, and our choices as we grow older confirm that fact. Yet, we're commanded to be righteous in order to dwell with God.

Why would God command us to do something we can't do? The answer is, *He doesn't.* For centuries before the birth of Christ, this heart-wrenching paradox and inner inability to keep the law were used to convict people of sin and point them toward a promised Savior. But when Jesus Christ came, He brought with Him the power to live a life between the lines. That's because our standard of righteousness now becomes inseparably linked to a crucial five-letter word: *faith.*

God Himself Brings Righteousness Within Our Reach

God knew we could never measure up to His righteous standards. That's why He instituted the shedding of blood of sacrificial lambs in the Old Testament and gave up His beloved Son, the Lamb of God, in the New Testament. That means that since the Cross, righteousness takes on a new meaning to Christians.

The apostle Paul put it this way: "Therefore by the deeds of the law there shall no flesh be justified in his sight: for by the law is the knowledge of sin. But now the righteousness of God without the law is manifested . . . *even the righteousness of God which is by faith of Jesus Christ*" (Rom. 3:20–22*a*, KJV, emphasis added).

How can we accomplish something that's beyond our ability? By putting our faith and trust in the One who through His Holy Spirit can give us the daily power to stay within the lines; to keep our lives, decisions, thoughts, and reactions on the straight and narrow; to keep His Word as an unvarying standard, even when it's hard to do.

The hardest work of bringing righteousness to a fallen world was done by Christ on the Cross. It is His righteousness that clothes, protects, confirms, and guides us. It's His shed blood that covers us from God's wrath in the days to come. But because God wants us conformed to the image of His Son right now, that's where we get to participate in making right choices—His choices.

In Psalm 15, David said that the second key to building an unshakable lifestyle is looking to God for the faith it takes to do what is right, even when it's difficult. Let's repeat that last sentence, because it's actually a part of our Trent-Hicks definition of the word *righteousness.*

Righteousness is choosing to have faith in Christ to give us the strength to do the right thing, even when it's difficult.

Faith can give us the power to walk the walk and talk the talk of a righteous life.

Lessons on Righteous Living

A seminary professor once asked his students this penetrating question: "Now that you don't have to do anything for your salvation, what are you going to do?" Take a moment to really think about it.

It's true that Christ alone paid for our salvation. But that doesn't mean we have nothing to do as Christians. In fact, because of what He's done for us, "what sort of people ought you to be in holy conduct and godliness?" (2 Pet. 3:11). Our love for and commitment to Christ for what He's done can more than motivate us to do what is right. With that motivation, how can we be righteous in our lives today?

If we group all the usages of *righteousness* in Scripture together, we can see three powerful primary aspects of right living:

1. Righteousness is shown in making God-honoring judgments.
2. Righteousness involves keeping our promises.
3. Righteousness compels us to tell the truth.

Those are three clear applications of righteous living, and all are found in Psalm 15. We'll devote entire chapters (chapters 10, 11, and 16) to the need to keep our promises and steadfastly maintain the truth. But in this chapter, we'll focus on the first aspect of righteousness: making God-honoring judgments in our daily lives.

Making a Habit of Making Godly Choices

Thirty-two times in Scripture, the words *righteousness* and *wickedness* are linked in the same sentence. That's because they carry opposite pictures of what God wants us to do. We've already seen that *righteous* means to "stay within the lines," to keep the standards God has set in our dealings with Him and others. What does *wickedness* mean? It means "to rebel against a standard, to walk away from a boundary." A related word for sin literally means "to miss the mark."

When we know the rules God has set and seek by faith to keep them even when it's difficult, we're working righteousness.

• Like the wife who stays with her husband when it would be so much easier to just walk away.

• Or the CPA who faces heat from his superiors but still turns out a true audit instead of just saying, "What do you want the balance to be?"

• Or the student who has the answers to the test in front of her, yet chooses to pass on the file folder instead of compromising her character.

Every day, a hundred times a day, we make choices. Sometimes they have no more to do with righteousness than peanut butter does with baseball. They're in the "Do I turn right or left?" or "What type of toothpaste should I buy?" category. But other times, they're a clear opportunity to choose what is right, even if it costs us.

And if we make a habit of making choices that honor the Lord—like turning off a raunchy television show, turning down an invitation to go to a wild party, or turning away from the opportunity to gossip—we're doing the solid work of building an unshakable lifestyle of righteousness. What's more, we're doing what Christ and His disciples did consistently—putting a sacrificial choice ahead of personal convenience.

It's not easy to work at righteousness. In fact, it takes plain, unadulterated courage—especially when doing what is right costs us that promotion, keeps us from turning in a false expense report we know will never be noticed, or forces us to confront an errant friend.

Exercising courageous faith to stay righteous keeps a woman from giving in to a worthless boyfriend's invitation to immorality, even if it means losing him. It keeps a man committed to the wife of his youth when a shameless woman at work seeks his attention and more. It keeps two parents of a special-needs child going "just one more day," and it gives that grandmother the conviction to reach out to others in her nursing home instead of holing up in her room.

The small, daily choices we make to do what is right, even when it's difficult, are what help us to "work righteousness." How can we develop the courage to keep doing what is right? One way is to look at the lives of those who have demonstrated courage in *big* ways. We can, for example, read *Through Gates of Splendor,* the incredibly inspiring story of Jim Elliot, a missionary who laid down his life for Christ. We can also look at the love and courage of a man named Andy who didn't hesitate to go above and beyond the call of duty in trying to do what was right for his friend.

The Hardest Choice

Andy Mynarski, the son of Polish immigrants, joined the Royal Canadian Air Force at the age of 27. In June 1944, he was the mid-upper turret gunner on a Lancaster bomber. On their thirteenth mission, Andy and his crew flew a late-night bomb run on the railroad yards at Cambrai, France, from their base in England.

As they neared the target, suddenly their plane was caught in a blinding flash. Soon other spotlights bathed the bomber in light, making it a sitting duck for anti-aircraft shells from below and German fighters from above.

The radio sprang to life as the tail gunner, Flight Lieutenant George

Patrick Brophy, yelled from his tiny cubicle at the end of the plane, "Six o'clock!" Fighters were coming in with their guns blazing, ripping holes in the fuselage, knocking out the port engines and starting a blaze of fire between Andy and his friend George.

Even in practice runs, Andy had refused to go back to the tail gunner position, saying, "Back there, you're completely cut off." And now his friend was cut off . . . literally.

The red light came from the pilot, indicating the crew must bail out. From his position in the tail, George Brophy saw white parachutes begin to fill the sky. That's when he pressed the rotation pedal to turn his turret so he could get out the rear door. But the hydraulic system had been shot out, freezing his turret in place.

Next he tried the hand crank that would turn the turret downward so he could just fall out—but the gear broke off. Now he was totally trapped, with the fire coming toward his end of the ship.

George looked up and saw Andy, who had made his way from the mid-turret to the rear escape hatch and was about to jump. Just then Andy glanced around and spotted his friend through the Plexiglas port of his turret. One look told Andy that George was trapped.

With the plane bucking violently, so much so that he couldn't stand, Andy got down on his hands and knees and crawled straight through the blazing hydraulic oil. By the time he reached the tail, his flying suit was on fire.

George tried to wave him away—shouting to him that it was hopeless—but still Andy desperately tried to work the turret free. It gave slightly, but not enough.

Seeing Andy on fire and helpless to rescue him, George yelled for him to get away, to save himself and bail out. Finally, reluctantly, Andy did crawl back to the door. Then he turned, saluted his friend, and bailed out.

Several minutes later, the flaming wreckage of the once-proud Lancaster smashed into a tree-lined field. In that last moment, the explosion of metal, trees, and ground snapped George Brophy's turret open, and he was thrown out of the plane and through the air. Miraculously, he woke up to find he'd survived the crash without a scratch!

Not so his friend.

In the days to come, George would learn the fate of his other crew members. One of the stories was of a parachutist who had landed alive, only to die later of severe burns. His flying helmet had had the word *Andy* painted across the front.

By choosing to ignore the flames and try everything he could to save his friend, Andy Mynarski gave his life. He received the Victoria Cross, the British Commonwealth's highest award for valor, and the lasting appreciation of his fellow airmen and country.

Andy's story is dramatic and heroic. It demonstrates a type of courage that few of us ever have to draw upon. But it also reminds us of the power of love that can cause us to do what is right, no matter the cost. It's the same call of love for Christ and our families and friends that causes us to look to God for the strength to do what's right—even if it costs us all we've got.

We saw how integrity can be the first, overall key to building an unshakable lifestyle. Now we've seen one way integrity is fleshed out through working righteousness. Our next stop is to look at another reflection of integrity, namely, a wonderfully freeing challenge to base our daily lives on truth.

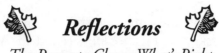 **Reflections**

The Power to Choose What's Right

1. In your own words, how do you define the term *righteousness?*

2. Think of someone who inadvertently (or purposely) blinded himself or herself to the white lines of God's Word. What were the consequences? How did you feel as you observed the situation?

3. Someone once said that "most of us go through life with chalk on our toes from standing too close to the line between right and wrong." Do you agree or disagree? Why?

4. Is there an area of your life where you have chalk on your toes? Is there an area where you've already crossed the line? What is it? What should you do about it?

5. What hard things do you face this week? Why not ask God to help you with them?

Chapter 9

THE THIRD KEY

The Freedom of a Truthful Walk

He . . . speaks truth in his heart.

Theres nothing like a spring wedding. On one beautiful April day, friends and family gathered around a happy couple. Everyone was dressed in the finest attire and wearing the biggest smiles.

As Vernon and Charmaine pledged their love to each other before God and those witnesses, it was a time of promise, hope, and warmth. They were a stunning couple who looked as though they had the whole world in the palms of their hands. The ceremony had been short but meaningful, and the reception was a time of best wishes, presents, and prayers of blessing.

During the service, Vernon had stood beside his bride and repeated after the minister, "I thee wed." But if the truth be known, as he held her hands, he should have looked her in the eyes and said, *"I thee wrong."* You see, Vernon had a little secret he was keeping—the fact that he was only separated, not divorced, from his previous wife. As devastating as that deception would be to his new bride when she found out, however, it was nothing compared to the series of lies that soon followed.

Vernon and Charmaine were married on April 23. On May 11, Vernon went to another wedding . . . not with Charmaine and not just to eat wedding cake, but to marry another woman, Jamillah.

Less than a month later, on June 5, Vernon was in yet another wedding, not as a groomsman but as the bridegroom, marrying his fourth wife, Lemitri.

Far from apologetic when finally exposed, Vernon used his lies to garner national attention, including appearances on three national talk shows. Even when he was convicted of bigamy and sent to prison for a short time, the deputy county attorney said he showed no remorse over his crimes.

Vernon's highly publicized lies hit the national papers, but they're not the only deceptions making headline news. Recently, we've seen the president of a major nonprofit corporation convicted of stealing hundreds of thousands of donated dollars to fund immoral relationships. And added to that are the everyday examples of corruption on nearly all levels of government.

Major lies often make major headlines. But dishonesty isn't something reserved for bigamists or politicians. There are thousands of unpublicized examples of dishonesty each day—from Christians and non-Christians alike. And while those individual acts of untruthfulness may never land a person on "Oprah," they place the people involved on shaky ground nonetheless.

Internal Aerobics

We've already seen in Psalm 15 that integrity and righteousness are inter-linking aspects of solid ground. David fit in a third element that can put our character on sure footing. *"He who . . . speaks truth in his heart."* This is also a third "aerobic exercise" designed to strengthen our hearts. We're to

walk with integrity,

work righteousness, and now

speak truth in our hearts.

As we look closely at this third key, we want to ask and answer, "What does it mean to speak truth in our hearts?" and "What are the benefits of a lifestyle based on truth?" We also want to look deeper into just *why* we're so prone to lie and what we can do to combat that temptation.

To begin, let's make sure we're clear on David's call to speak the truth in our hearts, for his words hold a two-part challenge.

Heart of Gold

In our modern culture, the "heart" describes a wide range of emotions and behaviors. Using the same word, we can add meaning such as "He has a big heart," referring to generosity; "She has a broken heart" to describe grief; or "I know deep down in my heart" or when talking about convictions— even, "My achy-breaky heart" or "She done stomped on my heart and mashed that sucker flat" when talking about country music.

The "heart" also has several meanings in Scripture, where it's a major concept. In the New International Version, for example, it's mentioned 546 times! And in addition to standing for the roughly three-pound physical organ that keeps one's blood moving, it's also pictured as the Grand Central Station of one's emotions, intellect, will, spirit, and soul. It stands for a person's character, decisions, compassion, and commitments. Here's a short look at other ways the heart is used:

- It is the source of speech (see Luke 6:45).
- It is the source of thoughts (see Matt. 15:19).
- It is the source of actions (see Matt. 15:19).
- It remembers (see Luke 2:51).
- It understands (see Matt. 13:15).
- It decides (see 2 Cor. 9:7, NIV).
- It is the source of emotions (see Acts 2:26).
- It is the source of one's relationship with God (see Acts 8:21).
- It believes God (see Rom. 10:9–10).
- It loves God (see Mark 12:30, 33).
- It is known by God (see Acts 1:24).

When God tells us to speak the truth in our hearts, He's pointing out that at the deepest level of our attitudes, thoughts, and actions, we're to put truth front and center. But was David calling us to speak the truth to others or to speak the truth to ourselves? If you said, "Both," you're right!

As we'll see, there are some who tell themselves lies regularly, undermining an honest sense of who they are in Christ. But it's also God's clear desire that we tell the truth to others. Why does truth-telling put such solid ground under our marriages, ministries, friendships, and professional careers? The answer is obvious, isn't it?

Perhaps it was in an earlier age, when your word was your bond, handshakes held huge business deals together, and cafeterias rarely missed a penny when food was paid for on the honor system. But in our day, when so many have gained so much from being so dishonest for so long, we need the reminder.

In our schools and even in many of our churches, absolute truth has been downgraded to individual opinions. And with the cultural confusion that results, we may be surprised how much a life based on truth is able to enrich and expand our enjoyment of life today.

To help us see truth's advantages, we'll look at five life-changing benefits of putting it at the center of our selves. Each benefit is important. But the fifth advantage qualifies us for one of the most incredible promises God has to offer.

> **We'll look at five life-changing benefits of putting truth at the center of our selves.**

After we've looked at these benefits, we'll consider why people are willing to lose so much by lying when they can gain so much by telling the truth. At least in part, the answer can be found in examining several lies recorded in Scripture—seeing what we can learn from them about what triggers untruthfulness—and how we can avoid those relationship killers.

With that in mind, let's look at the third key to a life that can never be shaken—the highly rewarding, daily commitment of speaking truth in our hearts.

Five Benefits of a Commitment to Truthfulness

When David called us to speak the truth, it was actually a command that carried with it several tremendous benefits. Benefits like . . .

1. Freedom from the Need to Maintain a Façade

At Forest Home Christian Conference Center, you'll find one of the top junior high camps in the country. It's called Lost Creek Ranch.[1] Just inside the entrance is a row of buildings that look like part of an old Western town. One is labeled "Hotel," and another has a big sign saying "Wells Fargo."

They look great on the outside! You think you've been transported back to the Wild West. But step inside and you've stepped into the future, not the past. Once you're beyond the thin façade, you won't find a boardinghouse lobby or see a Wells Fargo agent. Instead you'll find rooms that actually store equipment and provide modern housing for staff members and campers.

The outside of those buildings gives one message; the inside, something else. They make a great first impression, but that impression is independent of any internal reality.

In a similar way, many people today are "image managers."[2] They reject David's call to the solid ground of truthfulness and instead put up a façade that doesn't ring true. They project a one-inch-deep image before others. If someone were to peek behind the façade and see the substance of their actions and beliefs, the wooden props holding up the false front would come crashing down. And so, too, would their credibility and believability.

In our homes, workplaces, and even in political life, there's a predictable outcome when people feel tricked. *Anger.* For example, while we're not taking any particular political position, it's clear that the unprecedented changes our nation made on November 8, 1994, were due, at least in part, to tremendous anger in the electorate.

Many people saw politicians take clear stands on important issues during the 1992 campaign. Then when they began changing their stances once in office, at best they were looked at as "changeable," and at worst as deceptive.

The result? Anger.

The solution? A new image.

It's hard to believe, but in the aftermath of the 1994 election, *USA Today* ran a full-page feature on seven professional "image managers." These are experts in reshaping a politician's image. What an indictment of our system that this occupation even exists! Politicians don't need a *new* image. They need an image that doesn't shift like a house of mirrors. Their changing images were what largely sparked the anger in the first place.

Living a life of truthfulness means being the same person in public that we are in private. It means saying one thing when we're in Albany, California, and the same thing when we're in Albany, New York. Truthfulness involves projecting an image that isn't skin deep but bone deep. And such inner congruity can give us the kind of freedom that leads to a great night's sleep instead of staying up nights putting another coat of paint on a new façade.

2. Freedom from Being Found Out

As a second plus, being truthful gives a person incredible internal freedom. One clear example of this can be seen in the life of Abraham Lincoln. Though we look at Lincoln as one of the greatest presidents we've ever had, in his day he was often harshly criticized by the press and others. Some people despised him for his policy stands. Yet even to his critics, Lincoln was regarded as a man committed to truth.

When asked why he went to such great lengths to be accurate and honest, Lincoln answered, "I always tell the truth. That way I don't have as much to remember!"

Like the danger of falling façades, speaking one lie puts us in danger of adding a second . . . and a third . . . and a fourth just to make sure that the first lie is really covered up. And as we add lies (like Vernon in our opening story or even godly men like King David or Peter), each one greases the pole in a slippery slide toward a disrespected character.

3. Freedom from False Belief

The Bible teaches that who we are and what we believe determine how we live. Luke 6:45 puts it this way: "The good man out of the good treasure of his heart brings forth what is good; and the evil man out of the evil treasure brings forth what is evil; for his mouth speaks from that which fills his heart."

If God's truth has taken root in our hearts, we will live in the freedom of that truth. But if we believe things that aren't true, we'll be bound and limited.

You may remember the story of the ugly duckling. Because of an unfortunate mix-up, a swan's egg ended up in a duck's nest. When the eggs were hatched, the baby swan, as well as his duckling siblings and the mother duck, all believed him to be a duck, too. But because he didn't look like a proper duck, they considered him an ugly duckling. So he was treated badly, like an outcast, and developed a low opinion of himself.

One day, however, the young swan saw another swan, and he also saw a reflection of himself. Suddenly, he knew the truth about what he really was—a beautiful, graceful swan. He was then able to live according to that truth, and he enjoyed being the marvelous creature God made him to be.

Sometimes we build our lives on lies we believe to be true. Whether from ignorance or from choosing not to believe the truth when we hear it, the outcome is the same—bondage to those lies. Some people, for example, believe the lie that God doesn't love them, so they take every negative thing that happens as proof of their belief and discard any evidence that might indicate God *does* love them. It's vital that we know and live according to the truth. It frees us from façades, erases the fear of being found out, and breaks the chains of false beliefs.

4. Freedom from Guilt

King David, although he had a remarkable relationship with God and was mightily used by Him, was far from perfect. As great as his deeds for God were, his sins could be measured on a grand scale, too. His most infamous conduct came in his affair with Bathsheba and the subsequent cover-up scheme.

The greatest consequence for David was the effect the whole episode had on his relationship with God. In Psalm 32:3–4, he expressed the impact of his feelings of guilt: "When I kept silent, my bones wasted away through my groaning all day long. For day and night your hand was heavy upon me; my strength was sapped as in the heat of summer" (NIV).

For those who know the peace and joy of fellowship with God, guilt is painful, and rightly so. Just as physical pain is intended as a warning that something is wrong with our bodies, so guilt warns us that there is a spiritual problem in our lives.

David eventually responded to the pain of his guilt in Psalm 32:5: "Then I acknowledged my sin to you and did not cover up my iniquity. I said, 'I will confess my transgressions to the LORD'—and you forgave the guilt of my sin" (NIV).

When we don't speak the truth, we feel guilty and hamper our relationship with God. But when we speak the truth, we're relieved of that burden. In fact, even if what we lied about is "small" and insignificant, clearing it up by telling the truth can bring huge relief, just as it did for my (Rick's) friend Connie.

The Best Tip a Waitress Ever Picked Up

Connie, a waitress at a restaurant, took an order one day for a certain salad that required her to ask the customer what kind of cheese he wanted sprinkled on top. In the rush of having to take care of several tables, she forgot to ask the question. That became apparent as she was giving her order to the cook, who also happened to be her manager.

"What does he want on the salad?" he asked.

Not wanting her boss to know she had forgotten to ask, she blurted out, "Blue cheese."

Perhaps hearing some hesitation in her answer, he said, "Are you sure?"

"Yes, I'm sure," she lied, this time trying to put more certainty in her voice.

As it turned out, she had guessed correctly. As a result, no repercussions came from her boss or the customer. But that didn't mean there wasn't a cost. Inside, Connie was struggling.

Connie felt guilty about the lie, even though it seemed to be so small and harmless. Over the next few days, as she tried to have devotions, the memory of it kept nagging at her. Finally, she did something that was difficult but that led to one of the most freeing feelings she'd ever experienced. In order to clear her conscience, she went to the manager and told him what she had done.

It may have seemed like such a small thing. After all, she hadn't underreported her income by $20,000 or taken off from the scene of an injury accident. All she'd done is the same thing many people do every day—sometimes several times a day—tell a small, "white" lie. But that lie, and the unsettled feeling God's Spirit prompted inside as a result, made her feel as if her Christian life was as phony as those Western town fronts.

In as unhurried a moment as possible on her next shift, she spoke with the manager and apologized. At the time, he looked at her with piercing eyes but said little. After a hurried nod, he went about his business, and she went away feeling as if a 50-pound weight had been lifted off her shoulders.

Does telling the truth really pay off? We know all about the stories of government and industry whistle-blowers who received punishment, not rewards, for telling the truth. But inside, where Psalm 15 lays down the foundation stones of an unshakable life, telling the truth always pays off. And often it pays off in a more tangible way as well.

Several months later, the restaurant owner was looking to promote a waitress to a position of great trust: counting the money at the end of the night. Whom do you think he chose? Connie. She may have made a mistake. But by handling it in a godly way, she proved herself to be trustworthy. After all, a waitress who couldn't conceal a lie about a salad order was not going to steal his cash.

Connie enjoyed the peace of mind that comes from a clear conscience. (The extra money and promotion didn't feel bad either!) And it all came with the freedom, the absence of façades, and the release from guilt of a truthful character.

5. Turning God's Eyes Toward Us

As we mentioned above, the fifth benefit of speaking the truth involves one of God's most incredible promises. It's found in the Old Testament book of 2 Chronicles, and it tells us, "For the eyes of the LORD move to and fro throughout the earth that He may strongly support those whose heart is completely His" (2 Chron. 16:9).

God is actually *looking* for ways to strengthen and support us if we have truth in our hearts. He isn't merely sitting back and nodding His head approvingly. He's aggressively seeking ways to help those who choose to live out this element of Psalm 15.

I (Rick) had a boss at Biola University, Dr. J. Vincent Morris, who acted that way toward me. He was always looking for opportunities to encourage and develop me, both personally and professionally. I was a young dean, and I would often go off on a tangent, taking up the cause of a particular student group, or simply doing something that was inappropriate for that time or place. Dr. Morris was a couple of steps above me in the administrative hierarchy. Yet even though he wasn't my immediate supervisor, he always got word to me when I had done something right. And just as important, he lovingly counseled me to change direction if I was headed in the wrong direction.

Because of his active, positive interest in my role at the university, he added a welcome layer of confidence to my job. Because of his active interest in my life, I felt I had a guiding light that made sure I stayed on course and didn't wander onto rocky ground.

That's the kind of help God promises us in 2 Chronicles 16:9 (though on a much greater scale). When we speak truth in our hearts, we're walking on ground He walks on! We're reflecting His character. It's almost as if our lives are mirrors that get turned toward the sun, where they reflect a blinding display of God's life and love.

When King David told us in Psalm 15 that we're to speak truth in our hearts, it's a directive filled with everyday dividends. It even qualifies us for God's taking an added interest in our lives, the same thing He did in pursuing King David, "a man after God's own heart."

Why We Lie

We've looked at page after page of benefits we receive when we tell the truth. Yet, at times, we're still easily tempted to push the truth aside. Why? What motivates us to lie to ourselves and others when we stand to lose so much? In the Book of Genesis, we can find at least three reasons people lie. And let's face it: They aren't just examples stuck in the pages of history. They're traps we and our loved ones can fall into today.

1. We Lie to Avoid Consequences

The effort to avoid legitimate pain is one of the chief reasons for emotional and spiritual pain. Take one of our distant relatives, for example. In Genesis 3:4, "The serpent said to the woman, 'You surely shall not die!'" In this situation, Satan was tempting Eve to disobey God. He used that lie to deceive her into believing that eating the forbidden fruit would not have serious, lasting consequences. Eve trusted Satan rather than God—and later repeated the lie to Adam—because *she wanted to believe she could do as she pleased and not suffer any penalties.* All of us ever since have had the same desire.

Or take a look at another far-removed relation—our spiritual father Abraham. In Genesis 12:18–19, Pharaoh asked Abram, "Why did you not tell me that she [Sarah] was your wife? Why did you say, 'She is my sister'?"

Abram and Sarah had gone to Egypt to escape a famine in their land, and as they were on their way, Abram had made a strange request. He figured (correctly) that because of Sarah's great beauty, Pharaoh would want to take her as a wife. And Abram further assumed that he might be killed to make her available to Pharaoh. So to avoid any possible pain he might experience, he asked her to lie for him, to claim to be his sister, not his wife.

The plain fact is, whether it's Eve, Abraham, neighbor Ed, you, or I who lies, it may seem we're avoiding pain when we choose that course. But we're putting ourselves in danger of far greater pain when the lie is found out. To my discredit, I (John) learned this lesson the hard way years ago.

I was in junior high, and my brother Jeff and I had been invited to sleep over at a friend's house. Larry's home lay right on the edge of undeveloped land, and his parents had let him build a fort in the Arizona desert that backed up to their property. As this was decades ago and years before "stranger danger" would stop such a thing, we were allowed to sleep out in the fort as long as we didn't make too much noise.

From that fort, Larry, Jeff, six other friends, and I launched a late-night raid into a nearby neighborhood. Without asking permission or considering the right or wrong of the action, we did an amazing job of "papering" the house of a girl who went to our school.

We had just returned from our highly successful secret mission, and we were laughing about tissue-wrapping the trees and cars like mummies, when Larry's dad burst into the fort. "Where have you boys been?" he demanded angrily.

I froze, and fear hit me like a pail of cold water. But Larry did something that to my non-Christian way of thinking was remarkable. "Oh, Dad," he said with a smile, "calm down. We just went down to the 7-Eleven and got some snacks. See?" And he held up a bag of chips. "We just didn't want to wake you and Mom by barging into the house, but I should have come and asked you first. I'm sorry."

"Well . . . okay," his father said, his voice and face softening. "You're right, you should have asked me first. Now, you boys don't go outside the fort again until morning. Understand?"

"Yes, sir," Larry said. "We won't. See you in the morning."

I hate to admit it, but at the time I was incredibly impressed by what had taken place. One minute, it seemed we were in terrible trouble. The next instant, the trouble was gone. And it was all because of Larry's quick lie about going to the store (actually, the chips had been brought by one of the other guys) that fooled his dad and seemed to free us from the consequences of our actions.

Please understand that I didn't grow up in a Christian home, nor had I yet trusted Jesus as my Savior. At the time, all I could think was how effectively a lie could help you avoid punishment. I vividly recall that, as I went to sleep that night, I was thinking about how much I wanted to learn to lie like Larry.

Yet daylight has an unstoppable way of pushing back darkness . . . and exposing toilet-papered houses.

Convinced we were in the clear, all us boys trooped into Larry's house for breakfast—and there sat the father of the girl whose house we had decorated. After Larry's dad made each of us call our parents and tell them what we had done and how we had lied about it, this other father marched us over to clean up his house.

The lie Larry spoke (and to which we had all nodded in agreement at the time) kept the consequences away for a few hours, but it ended up doubling the punishment for each of us when the truth was finally revealed. That's the deceptive nature of thinking that lies can push problems away or keep us from experiencing "biting" consequences. Let me explain further.

Why Lies Are Easier to Pick Up Than Put Down

My (John's) good friend Gary Richmond is a former zoo curator and currently a pastor to single parents in California. He has also written one of my favorite books called *A View from the Zoo*. In it, he tells incredible true stories of working with animals of all sorts in over 10 years at the Los Angeles Zoo.

One story Gary tells (and that sends chills down my spine when I hear him describe it in person) is about the time they had to "milk" the king cobra that was having problems molting its skin. Picture an eight-foot-long king cobra with a bite so deadly that it has been known to kill an elephant that wandered too near! Then picture this snake in molting season, when the old skin gets snagged on the scar tissue around its eyes!

It doesn't take much imagination to see in your mind's eye a deadly snake shaking its head, trying to get rid of its old skin that won't slide off. Now consider the courage it took for the zoo's herpetologist and several *volunteers* like Gary to go into the cage and help the cobra shed its skin.

It took several grown men to capture and hold the snake, with Gary being responsible for holding it right behind its head while the vet milked the snake of venom. (They did that so that if any of the helpers were bitten, the reduced amount of venom might make it possible for that unfortunate person to live long enough to get help!) The whole scene is something you must read for yourself to capture the sheer terror of being that close to a deadly reptile. Yet what Gary learned from that experience is something we can all learn from as well.

After they had surgically removed the snake's skin, tossed the snake as far away from them as possible, and run to safety outside the cage, Gary made a logical statement. He mentioned to the vet with great emotion how fortunate they'd been to catch the snake without being struck. And that's when the vet told him a chilling fact. "Gary," he said, "most people don't get bit picking up a snake but *putting it down.*"

It was easy for Eve to reach up and disobey God by picking the apple. It was impossible to later try to put it down. It was easy to try to blame her decision on her husband, but it didn't prevent her from being struck by sin and incredible consequences.

The same thing is true with the person who ignores the truth of God's Word and commits adultery . . . or steals . . . or begins a series of lies. Those acts may be easy initially to pick up, but they cost us mightily when we try to put them down. Like a crooked land deal, lying looks as if it offers the payoff of a lifetime. But it sells us a lie and leaves us with swampland in Louisiana, not Malibu beachfront property.

2. We Lie to Avoid Responsibility

In Genesis 4:9, Cain told God, "I do not know [where my brother, Abel, is]. Am I my brother's keeper?"

The short answer to Cain's question was yes, he was his brother's keeper. Yet Cain had murdered Abel out of jealousy because God had accepted Abel's offering but not Cain's. When God asked Cain His question, part of Cain's lie showed how he wanted to deny he was responsible for others.

I (John) remember an experience when I was a Young Life leader years ago. There was a non-Christian boy named Brian who had been joyriding in his parents' car without permission (and under age) and had been thrown in jail. When he couldn't reach either of his parents at home, he called me in desperation.

I'll never forget his father's response when I finally tracked him down at his place of work. "Brian's in jail?" he asked, dumbfounded. "If he's in jail, he isn't *my* son. I'm not talking to him. You call his mother."

What he said was a lie. Brian *was* his son. His flesh and blood was in a holding cell. And trying to deny responsibility for his son's action and his own participation in the problem didn't change the facts.

Lying doesn't help us avoid legitimate pain, nor does it abdicate our responsibility for doing what's right.

3. We Lie When We Think God Isn't Going to Meet Our Needs

Jacob and Esau were twins as different as night and day. Esau was a man of the field, Jacob a man of the tents. Esau was a tanned, hairy outdoorsman and hunter. Jacob was a pale, smooth-skinned, stay-at-home kid. Yet they both wanted the same thing—their father's blessing.

But while they both wanted it, only one had been given God's promise he would receive it. That was Jacob, the younger, who God had prophesied would be the ruler of his older brother.

So what's this? Jacob wondered one day. Their old, nearly blind father was sending Esau out to hunt game and return with a hot, savory meal before he was to receive the blessing that was supposed to have been reserved for Jacob. If you're familiar with this story in Genesis 27, you'll remember that while Esau was out hunting, a more crafty hunter came into his father's tent. Jacob had dressed up in Esau's smelly hunting clothes and had even put animal pelts on his hands so his smooth skin wouldn't give him away.

When Jacob's voice almost betrayed him, however, his father asked him how he had come back so quickly. Then he asked Jacob point-blank, "Are you really my son Esau?"

Jacob lied and said, "Yes, I am."

The rest is biblical history. And though the younger son did receive the blessing as was foretold, he gained it not by faith but by trickery. Jacob knew God had said he was to receive his father's blessing, yet when push came to shove, he certainly didn't display the faith of his grandfather Abraham. When it looked as though a "need" would slip away, Jacob took matters into his own hands.

A modern-day Jacob named Jannie also took matters into her own hands when she thought a need was going unmet. She had held out for God's best until she was 27 years old. Then fear of her biological clock ticking down led her to take dramatic action. She started going to nightclubs instead of church, accepting the lie that this was a legitimate way to fulfill her desires. She did find a young man to marry her . . . but he divorced her less than a year later. Now she's back in church. Only this time it's as a single parent filled with hurt from not trusting God to meet a deep-felt need.

There was nothing wrong with Jannie wanting to be married. Yet at the heart of sin is trying to meet a legitimate need in an illegitimate way. Our lack of faith in God's ability or willingness to act on our behalf can cause us to take matters into our own hands—to try to meet our own needs in our own way—and to think that living out that lie won't bring severe consequences.

In an Age of Deception, How Do We Fill Our Lives with Truth?

We've seen a few of the benefits of truthfulness in this chapter, as well as a few common reasons why it's so tempting to choose lies instead. But if we want to "stack the deck" in favor of telling the truth, how can we increase our commitment to truth and then live out that commitment? In the next chapter, we'll present three biblical tools that will help transport truth deep inside our hearts.

# *Reflections*
The Freedom of a Truthful Walk

1. Think of a time when you or someone else was caught in a lie. How did you or the other person feel? Were you or the other person able to rebuild the trust of those to whom the lie was told?

2. John and Rick list five benefits of a commitment to truthfulness (pp. 80-85). How important are those freedoms to you personally? Which one do you value the most?

3. Recall the story of the ugly duckling. What are the results of someone believing a lie about himself or herself?

4. When you know you've done something wrong, how does it make you feel? What do you do to resolve the guilt?

5. Reread 2 Chronicles 16:9. On a scale of 1 to 10 (1 being "My heart belongs only to me" and 10 being "My heart is totally devoted to God"), how much does your heart belong to God? What can you do to move it up a notch or two?

6. Think of examples of how God has strongly supported you when you've been completed devoted to Him. How did you feel when that occurred?

7. Reread the three reasons we lie found in the Book of Genesis (pp. 85-90). Which reason for lying do you struggle with the most? Why?

 *Chapter 10*

Feeding on Truth

He who . . . speaks truth in his heart . . .

Right in Scripture are three powerful methods for placing truth in the center of our hearts. If the last chapter points out the whys of speaking truth, this chapter provides the how-tos that lead us to the solid ground of Psalm 15. They begin with the need to paint a "picture" of truth in our hearts.

Hanging a Picture of God's Truth in Our Hearts

Sharon just couldn't get the picture. It's not that she didn't know the truth. The truth was that she was an attractive, generous, loving, God-fearing woman.

Yet she never saw herself that way.

The truth was that she'd been married for 22 years to a wonderful Christian man who had loved her from the first day he met her. God had given them two precious daughters, each well adjusted and doing extremely well in a Christian college.

Yet she never felt truly loved by any of them.

Like trying to push a huge boulder up a hill, Sharon would try and try to convince herself that she really was valuable. That she mattered to God and her family. That her husband really did love her for who she was as a person deep inside. But each time she got close to the top of the hill, those memories of her grinning, heartless, alcoholic father would flood back, and that giant stone would roll all the way down to the bottom.

Like many victims of physical and sexual abuse, Sharon had a "frozen" place inside her heart. The shame and conflicting emotions of what had happened made her feel as if her childhood had been robbed and she was somehow flawed inside. She felt so flawed, in fact, that she was convinced that if people really knew the "truth"—really knew the dark secrets she held—they wouldn't love her. They *couldn't* love her, because the "truth" she saw deep inside was that she was unlovable. And that misbelief kept her pushing that stone up the hill and having it roll back down again.

Certainly, it had helped when she'd become a Christian. Now she knew the truth that Jesus cared for her immensely. He was aware of every detail of her childhood hurt, and He loved her absolutely, accepted her unconditionally, and cleansed her completely.

Yet she never felt truly acceptable even in His sight. That is . . . until one day when truth crashed home in her heart.

It wasn't something she learned in one of her many counseling sessions. Nor did she read it in a self-help book. It came when she got an unexpected "picture" of an irrefutable truth, first with her husband and then with her Lord.

It happened the day that Sharon and Alan, her husband, were renewing their insurance policies. A nurse from the insurance company came to their home early one morning to draw their blood and give Alan an EKG (an electrocardiogram test, which measures a person's heart rate and rhythms).

Sharon went first and had the nurse draw her blood. He was unusually proficient at the task, so Sharon barely flinched when he found a vein. Sharon then went back to the bedroom to shower and get ready to go to a women's Bible study, and Alan took his turn having his blood drawn and getting his EKG.

Alan was lying on a couch in the family room, in the middle of his test, when Sharon walked into the adjoining kitchen. From where the nurse had positioned him, Alan could see his wife.

"You sure clean up good, honey," he said with a smile.

"Thanks," Sharon said without giving her husband's words a second thought. After all, he had said nice things like that ever since they'd been married . . . but she'd never really heard them.

When his EKG was over, Alan walked back to their bedroom to get cleaned up. And that's when it happened. Like a 100-pound anvil falling on her foot, Sharon had a "picture" crash through all those years of disbelief, shattering walls of self-protection and opening a pathway for God's truth to come in.

As the nurse finished putting away the EKG machine and was gathering his things, he stopped and said to Sharon, "By the way, your husband really loves you."

"Why . . . thank you," she said, slightly embarrassed and not knowing exactly what had prompted that observation.

The nurse stood there looking at her for a moment and then said, "I can prove it to you."

"You can do *what?*" Sharon asked.

"I can prove to you that your husband loves you," he said without a hint of sarcasm or jesting.

Since her earliest memories, Sharon had wanted to truly know someone loved her. Irrefutably. Uncompromisingly. Thousands of times she'd wanted to be able to prove to herself that Alan did love her, to move his love from her head to her heart. How could this stranger offer such a gift?

"Look at this," he said, laying the strip of paper that came out of the EKG machine in front of her.

Before her was a series of lines made by a marking needle like those you've seen in every doctor movie and every police show in which a lie detector was used.

"This is where your husband's heartbeat and blood pressure were during the first half of the test," he said, pointing to a long stretch of similar lines, all at relatively the same height. "And this is when you walked into the room."

There it was, in black and white. *Irrefutable. Uncompromised. Unquestionable.*

"See how his heartbeat and blood pressure went way up when he saw you and then when he spoke to you? And this is how it went back down to where it had been when you walked out of the room."

A waterfall of emotions fell on Sharon. Her eyes filled with tears, and she ran down the hall to their bedroom. She sobbed uncontrollably for almost half an hour, much of that time with Alan holding her, trying to comfort her and find out what was wrong. Actually, at long last, she was crying tears of joy about what was *true.*

When Sharon told me (John) this story, she was convinced that God had given her the very thing she needed—a picture of her husband's love that would prove beyond a shadow of a doubt that he really meant what he said. Now she plans to frame it and hang it on the wall. And even better still, that experience opened the way for pictures of *God's* love to fill her heart as well.

It shouldn't surprise us that a picture can be such a powerful tool for reinforcing truth and combating disbelief, because God has used pictures the same way throughout His Word. If you want to center truth in your heart, or if you struggle with deep-seated misbeliefs or with telling yourself or others the truth, try looking up and lingering over some of the hundreds of pictures of God's love recorded there. For example:

> - A good shepherd who leads us by quiet waters (see Ps. 23:1-2)
> - The father of a prodigal who keeps the lights of home always lit (see Luke 15:11-32)
> - A solid fortress we can run to in times of trouble (see Ps. 18:2)
> - The "suffering servant" who gives His life for His sheep (see Isa. 53)
> - A loving Guide who gives us light for our path (see Ps. 119:105)
> - The Captain who fights to secure our salvation (see Heb. 2:10, KJV)
> - A bright morning star to guide us (see 2 Pet. 1:19)

We don't claim to understand all that happens in the process of reflecting long and often on these pictures of who God is and His love for us, but we do know it moves truth further into our hearts, particularly when we also use a second tool: biblical meditation.

Meditation . . . God's Way

When I (Rick) was working in Hollywood in the 1960s, I would often drive by a billboard that pictured a giant guru dressed in long, white robes whose title was Swami. He had long, white hair and a flowing beard, and he was pictured sitting, with his legs crossed, looking mellow and at peace. The bold headline under the picture intrigued me: "Come and learn to meditate."

Now, that caught my interest. You see, I wasn't a Christian at the time, but like a lot of young people in that era, I was still curious about spiritual things . . . even Eastern mystical concepts. Driving by that billboard day after day, I grew more and more intrigued. *Maybe there's something to this meditation stuff,* I began to think. *After all, the Beatles have their own guru.*

Finally, I'd seen his face on that billboard long enough. I decided that the next day, I'd go to one of the introductory meetings it advertised.

About 20 people gathered at the appointed time and sat in a circle of chairs, waiting to meet the swami and be enlightened. But instead of the robed one, in walked a swami assistant who explained all the benefits we could expect from Eastern meditation *if* we took his classes.

"It will help you to relax and get rid of stress," he said. "It will help you to think more clearly and creatively in school or on the job." On and on he went, describing all the wonderful things meditation was supposed to do for us.

What he *didn't* explain, of course, was *how* to do the meditation. In order to learn that, we would need to come back the *next* day. And if we did come back, we would have to be wearing clean clothes (a real switch for a lot of young people in those days). We would also need to bring fresh fruit, fresh flowers, a clean handkerchief—and oh, there was that 45 bucks we needed to bring, too.

I was hooked. It all sounded too good to be true (which should have been a warning right there). I was ready to find some peace in my life, and I committed myself to giving it a try. I came back the next day in clean clothes, with my fruit, flowers, hanky, and cash in hand. Then in walked a normal-looking guy who turned out to be the instructor. He began to describe the nuts and bolts of Eastern meditation.

As I sat there, smelled the incense, listened, and tried the exercises, I realized that the meditation they were presenting was really a form of self-hypnosis. Soon I realized that not only was I *not* going to meet the real swami on the billboard, but I wasn't going to find any spiritual benefit for me or anyone else, either! Disappointed, I gave up on meditation and considered myself wiser but $45 poorer.

Imagine how shocked I was years later when as a new Christian I discovered that meditation isn't just something for swamis and their students. There's actually such a thing as *biblical* meditation. In fact, it's commanded for all the saints in Scripture. (See, e.g., Josh. 1:8: "This book of the law shall not depart from your mouth, but you shall meditate on it day and night. . . .")

As I began to study biblical meditation, I discovered that it is, indeed, a powerful tool for taking truth and moving it front and center in our hearts. In fact, meditating on God's Word (and His word pictures like the one above) provides a potent "delivery system" that puts even more of God's truth, wisdom, and light into our inner beings.

Delivery system?

Scientists are continually perfecting better ways to "deliver" something. Years ago, for example, if you wanted extra vitamins, you'd have to eat extra fruits or vegetables. Then came the vitamin pill, an easier, faster way to deliver the vitamins. And recently, nutritional researchers introduced "spray vitamins" that speed an even higher percentage of those healthy vitamins throughout a person's body.

Meditation is a God-ordained delivery system that can place more of the good things of the Bible into our hearts. But what is it? Believe it or not, we can gain the clearest picture of what it is by taking a trip to a meadow and observing one of God's lowliest (but coolest) creatures.

Meditation . . . in a Meadow!

When I (Rick) was a small boy, I spent every summer in Kentucky on my great-grandparents' farm. One of my jobs, as the youngest member of the family, was to go out every day and count the cows. There were more than 50 in the herd. If one was missing, I would ring the bell, and we would hop on the tractors to go find it. After doing that job for a number of summers, I became a pretty good student of cow behavior.

In case you haven't noticed, cows are about the coolest animal in the barnyard crowd. They walk around nonchalantly and don't get shaken up by too many events of the day—unlike such uncool animals as chickens. Chickens walk around as if they have some sort of shaking disease. They have wings, but they can't fly. And they pick at things with their beaks that you don't want to step in.

But cows are cool. They go to bed early and get up early. And when they get up, the first thing they usually want is a little water. Cows are sensible about that. They'll walk right into a lake, about chest deep. Then they just have to open their mouths to get their water.

After they drink, it's time for something to eat. Cows are smart about the way they do that, too. When they eat grass, they take the grass with their lips, tear it off at ground level, and eat. They leave the roots in the ground to continue growing. When the cows come back the next day or the next week, that grass will still be there, and they can eat more of it. (Sheep, on the other hand, will pull up grass by the roots and leave nothing to grow, so there's no grass to come back to another day.)

After drinking, eating, and being kind of social, cows sit down together and take a little rest. Then about lunchtime, instead of going out and getting a whole new meal of grass, one cow will say to another, "Let me bring up a good idea."

Now, right here you need to know that in addition to being quadrupeds, cows are also "quadruguts," meaning they have four stomachs. And when they have breakfast, they fill up tummy number 1. You also need to know that although grass is nutritious for cows, it's hard to digest, and the process takes a long time. So, when the cows get hungry again, instead of getting up to eat other food, they just bring up into their mouths the grass that's still in stomach number 1. They chew on it again for a while, and when they're finished, they swallow and *plop*—it goes down into stomach number 2.

(Trust me . . . this has a lot to do with meditation!)

The same process will happen when it's time for dinner. Instead of eating more grass, the cows will bring the remaining grass up from stomach number 2 and chew on it a while longer, getting still more nutrition out of it. When they're done, the grass goes into stomach number 3.

Later, when it's time for the final meal of the day, the same process happens all over again. The cows will chew and grind even more nutrients out of the grass. Then it goes to stomach number 4, after which it may become a meadow muffin. We go around and gather the muffins to put on our roses because there's still nutrition in them for the flowers.

Chewing on God's Word

Why describe the slightly unappetizing eating and digestive process of cows? Because the word for *meditation* used in Joshua 1:8 is the same Hebrew word that's used to mean "a cow chewing its cud." In other words, what the cow does to the grass is what we're to do with God's Word . . . figuratively speaking, of course.

As the cow fills its stomach with grass, we're to study God's Word and store it in our minds. Then, at a later time, we can retrieve the Word and "chew" on it some more. We can break it down further with the help of the Holy Spirit, who teaches us; in the process, we get more nutrition from it. Far from exhausting the nutritional value of a passage by bringing it to mind time and again, the Word of God is so rich that we could take years to study just one verse (or write an entire book on just five verses in a psalm).

As various situations arise, or as we have time to think during the day, we can bring up God's Word and get additional nutrition from it. And the more of it we have stored in our minds, the more of it we can meditate on, and the more likely we'll be to prosper in God's economy. In fact, we'll have God's thoughts in our minds all the time. Then when we need to make decisions, we won't necessarily need to sit and think about what's right or wrong from God's perspective. We'll know how He would want us to respond.

J.I. Packer, in his classic book *Knowing God*, gives us further insight into what meditation is all about. He defines it as:

> the activity of calling to mind, and thinking over, and dwelling on, and applying to oneself, the various things that one knows about the works and ways and purposes and promises of God.
>
> It is an activity of holy thought, consciously performed in the presence of God, under the eye of God, by the help of God, as a means of communion with God.
>
> Its purpose is to clear one's mental and spiritual vision of God, and to let His truth make its full and proper impact on one's mind and heart.[1]

Need an everyday example of how meditating on a passage of Scripture can make a tremendous difference in a person's life? How about a heroic one? In fact, the most heroic act of the First World War might well have never happened if it hadn't been for one man meditating for two days on God's Word and finally hearing God's clear direction for his life.

On October 8, 1918, in the trenches of France, Corporal Alvin York of the United States was ordered to take a reconnaissance patrol out to note the position of a series of German machine gun nests. The enemy spotted their advance, however, and began pouring small arms fire down on York and his men.

Within moments, every man in his patrol except York was either killed or wounded. Seeking to protect his men, York crawled under intense fire to a flanking position and began pouring round after round from his rifle into the German troops filling a trench. He killed 25 Germans as he advanced from machine gun nest to machine gun nest. Finally, in desperation, the next group of German soldiers threw up their hands in surrender.

York had captured a major among those men, and York ordered the officer at gunpoint to yell for all of his men to surrender. Nearly 30 men stood up, and York single-handedly began marching them back to the Allied lines.

Along the way, other German soldiers, seeing one man leading so many troops, assumed the entire line had collapsed and began surrendering to York in droves.

When this Tennessee mountain man finally reached the American field headquarters, he had 132 prisoners to turn in. Along the way, he had recruited only three other American soldiers to help.

Although every Allied nation honored York for his incredible heroism, what few people knew was that Alvin York had once been a conscientious objector to the war.

As a youth, York had been a rabid drinker and fighter. But then, in a dramatic conversion, he became a Christian and turned over a whole new leaf. He held closely to Scripture, including the passages that said, "You shall not kill." That's why, when his draft notice came in 1917, he at first refused to report. Then he agreed to enter the service only if he could be marked a conscientious objector—someone they wouldn't send to the front.

Shortly before York and his unit were to be shipped overseas, however, a wise commanding officer sensed York's inner struggle. York wasn't seeking to avoid combat because he was a coward but because of his convictions. So the commander gave York a two-day pass to go home, read his Bible, *meditate on God's Word,* and then come back with his decision. Once he'd meditated and prayed over the decision, his superior would honor his choice either way—to fight or not to fight.

What did York meditate on those two days? Primarily Romans 13. And after meditating for those two days on God's Word . . . *chewing and chewing* . . . he made up his mind. As God had placed the civil authorities under His power, so he, Alvin York, would obey their call to war, not to take lives but to save them. And on that dreadful, heroic day in October 1918, he saved the lives of hundreds of American soldiers who would have walked into those enemy machine gun nests. A conscientious objector stood on that ground in France and won the Medal of Honor because he had meditated on God's Word.

High on the List of a Righteous Man

Thankfully, as I write this, none of us face the immediate challenge of fighting in a world war. But the decisions we have to make—from what job to take, to what church to join, to which school our kids should attend—can all be meditated on. Prayed over. Lingered over to hear not only the world's or our friends' advice, but even more important, God's quiet voice amid the clamor.

We've already seen, in the second key to anchoring our lives in solid ground, that we're to work righteousness. And in Scripture, one clear attribute of a righteous person is his or her commitment to meditating on God's Word. Psalm 1 contrasts a righteous man with a wicked man. And high on the list of a godly man's traits is "his delight is in the law of the LORD, and in His law he meditates day and night." The psalm goes on to say that the individual who meditates on God's Word "will be like a tree firmly planted by streams of water, which yields its fruit in its season, and its leaf does not wither; and in whatever he does, he prospers."

In other words, when we delight in God's Word and meditate on it, we send down deep roots. We also ensure plenty of "water"—supplied by the source of "living water" Himself. And, in God's timing, we bear fruit. That is, we're productive in what God has planned for us.

We can look to Psalm 119:97–100 for another list of benefits of meditating on God's Word: We'll be wiser than our enemies, have more insight than our teachers, and gain more understanding than the aged.

But doesn't meditating take a lot of time? Yes, it does. In an age when we want instant everything, it's easy to think that we can be "one-minute" Christians as well as "one-minute" managers. But it's not true. It takes time and effort to place God's Word deep into our hearts.

I (John) remember perhaps the most life-changing class I took in seminary. It was taught by Dr. Zane Hodges, a godly professor and pastor of an inner-city church in Dallas. I'll never forget his instructions the first day of class.

We had all signed up to take a class on the Book of Hebrews. It was a Greek class in which we would translate the book, breaking it down bit by bit in the original language. And if that wasn't challenging enough, Dr. Hodges added another stipulation: "Men, as a part of the class requirements, I'd like you to spend one hour on Monday, Wednesday, and Friday simply meditating on God's Word in the Book of Hebrews. Not translating it. Not studying *about* it. But quietly, prayerfully, picking a single passage and meditating on it."

I can remember the first Monday I faced my required hour of meditation. I thought. I prayed. I reflected. And then I prayed about what I'd do for the next 59 minutes.

Try it! Take *one solid hour* out of your week to meditate on what God would say to you through a passage of Scripture. I gradually got much better at it, and the benefits for me, and for anyone who will take the time to meditate, are tremendous. To help you make the hour productive, here are three suggestions I was given by Dr. Hodges that I still use today:

1. Set aside a quiet place where you can focus your thoughts on God's Word.

For Alvin York, it was climbing a mountainside in Tennessee. For you, it may be getting up a half hour early or taking a lunch to work and closing the door when everyone else has left the office. In as quiet a place as possible, try to tune out the noise and distractions of the day and focus your attention on God's Word and what He has to say to you through it.

2. Prayerfully, carefully, read through a passage, lingering over each word.

According to 2 Timothy 3:16, "All Scripture is inspired by God." That means the very words of the Bible are divinely inspired and profitable for teaching, reproof, and correction. Linger over each word in the passage you've picked, asking God to fill your heart with meaning and insight.

3. Use this opportunity to turn the words of Scripture into a prayer for you or your loved ones.

For example, if the passage you picked is one dealing with trusting God with our fears (e.g., "Be anxious for nothing, but in everything by prayer and supplication with thanksgiving let your requests be made known to God" [Phil. 4:6]), after you've carefully thought and prayed through each word, seek to apply the message directly to your life. You could take Philippians 4:6 and pray, "Lord, help me today to be anxious about nothing. Make me a person of prayer who continually brings my supplications before You. I thank You for inviting me to make my needs known to You. And I thank You for caring so much about those needs."

After you've prayed the passage for yourself, you can do the same for your spouse or child: "Lord, help my mate (or child) today to be anxious about nothing. Make him (or her) a person of prayer who brings all supplications to You."

What we're focusing on here is not in any way rewriting Scripture but applying it. And if you try this method, you'll see that praying Scripture can be a powerful way to build God's truth into your heart and weave more of His words into the fabric of your loved ones' lives as well.

We've looked at two tools for taking in truth—studying the pictures of God's love and character in His Word and biblical meditation, which can deeply implant His truth in our hearts. There's also a third crucial tool we'd like to offer.

A "Memory-Challenged" Practical Memory System

Another way to be actively involved in the process of internalizing Psalm 15 and the stability it offers is to *memorize* God's Word. You could start today and in just a few minutes memorize all five verses of this psalm.

Memorize an entire psalm? You say you'd like to memorize God's Word but don't have a good memory?

Though most of us feel "memory challenged" when it comes to memorizing Scripture, we can master the technique if we have a practical plan to follow.

We're convinced that if you're serious about putting truth in your heart, you'll put God's Word in your heart. That's because Scripture says in no uncertain terms, "Thy word is truth." What's more, though most of us feel "memory challenged" when it comes to memorizing Scripture, we can master the technique if we have a practical plan to follow . . . like the one my (Rick's) good friend Dave Hopkins has developed.

Dave worked alongside me at Forest Home Christian Conference Center. During his 20-plus years of ministering there, one of his main areas of focus was discipling the college students who worked for him during the summer. With a long, grueling camp season, it was absolutely necessary to maintain positive, loving attitudes among those students. And as a main tool for doing that, Dave would encourage his staff to memorize Scripture. In fact, he set up a practical, effective memory system that he taught for years. Some of those summer staff went into full-time ministry, the rest went into various other fields, but all took Dave's method for memorizing Scripture with them. With his permission, we'd like to show his method to you as well.

Eight Steps to Memorizing God's Word

1. If you've never memorized God's Word before, don't tackle too many verses at once.

It's easy to get overwhelmed after a few days or weeks, and you might want to give up. So, start with just one or two verses a week.

2. Memorize from a translation that you can easily understand and use every day.

3. Discipline yourself from the beginning to say each verse word for word.

This is important! If you don't do it, you'll probably forget the verse or continue to paraphrase it more and more. This may seem a little compulsive, but if you allow yourself to be sloppy and learn something other than what's written, you take the chance of misquoting the Bible to yourself and others.

4. Use repetition as the key.

As an example of how to use repetition to memorize, take Psalm 15:

    a.   Read the first sentence three times:
        "Lord, who may abide in Thy tent?"
    b.   Then, without looking, try to say the first sentence three times.
    c.   Next read and say the second sentence three times by itself:
        "Who may dwell on Thy holy hill?"
    d.   Say the two sentences together three times:
        "Lord, who may abide in Thy tent? Who may dwell on Thy holy hill?"
    e.   Continue adding phrases or sentences until you've memorized what you want to learn that day.

5. Review, at least once every day, all previously learned verses.

6. Realize that it takes nearly five weeks of doing something each day for it to become a habit.

That's true whether you're breaking an old habit or starting a new one. So, give yourself at least a month to begin to learn the discipline of Scripture memorization. Psalm 15 is a great place to start.

7. Use as many of your senses as possible.

Seeing, hearing, writing, and speaking all help to engrave a verse in your mind. Be creative! The very act of writing it down on 3x5 cards for learning and later reviewing is helpful for many. Dave Hopkins says a verse into a microcassette recorder, plays it back, and reads along as he's hearing what he memorized. This is a way he can speak, hear, and read God's Word simultaneously while checking to make sure he has said it verbatim. (A tape recorder tells no lies.)

Another creative way of learning Scripture is to put it to music. This is something Dave did for more than 20 years while working with junior-high students at Forest Home. He would have the music team teach them verses set to music (like the original psalms), keeping them as short and catchy as possible for quick learning and yet verbatim with Scripture. In one week, students would easily learn six or more verses!

8. As a form of accountability, write in a notebook or your Bible the date when you begin memorizing a verse, sentence, or paragraph of Scripture.

Work on memorization for a week, keeping that written account. It'll be a good reminder to review and an encouragement to see all that you've been able to store in that brain of yours. You'll be amazed at what you can learn and retain. If you continue to review your verses day after day, you will be treasuring God's Word in your heart (see Ps. 119:11). New verses and chapters will become easier to memorize, and entire books will become attainable!

You can do it!

If you take the time to look at the many pictures of God's character and truth in Scripture, meditate in an unhurried and prayerful way on His Word, and then spend time memorizing it for instant access, you'll be well on your way to anchoring your life in truth—and in the same rock-solid ground God Himself walks on. What's more, you'll be ready to take on the challenges of the next set of three keys to an unshakable lifestyle—three relationship killers we must avoid.

Reflections

Feeding on Truth

1. When you hear the word *meditation,* what images come to mind?

2. Reread J.I. Packer's definition of meditation on page 100. Have you ever meditated on God's Word? What started you on that process? What results did you see in your life?

3. Read the benefits of meditating on Scripture found in Psalms 1:2–3 and 119:97–100. Which of those would be most beneficial to your life?

4. Why not commit yourself to meditating on Psalm 15 this week, using the three suggestions described on page 103? When and where do you plan to do this?

5. Of the eight steps for memorizing God's Word, which do you find the easiest? The most difficult?

6. Whom could you begin to memorize Scripture with? Why not ask that person to join you in memorizing Psalm 15 today?

7. Think of a struggle in your life or a decision you need to make that you could help resolve by memorizing key verses on the subject and meditating on them.

They Protect Our Most Important Relationships

Chapter 11

THE FOURTH KEY

Avoiding Interpersonal Espionage

He does not slander with his tongue.

W e've seen the first three stepping-stones in our search for solid ground. As we continue our study of Psalm 15, we'll see that David made two major shifts as he described the next three elements of an unshakable lifestyle.

First, he changed our focus from looking inside at our heart attitudes and actions to looking outward toward how we treat our loved ones and friends. He also turned from telling us three things to *add* to our lives to naming three things we need to *erase* from our everyday actions.

That's a big switch as we begin this new section of Psalm 15. And it's one that can help us build up our relationships by not tearing them down.

Sticks and Stones and Slander

What's the first thing David told us to avoid like the plague? Try interpersonal espionage.

Try what?

From Mata Hari to James Bond to our daily news, we've all grown accustomed to hearing about *international* espionage. At the time of this writing, for example, headlines still surface regularly about the Aldrich Ames spy case. It's the tragically true story of a top CIA agent who turned traitor a few years ago. He went through hundreds of thousands of dollars and ended the lives of dozens of covert agents by selling secrets to the Soviets.

That's a tragedy, all right. But what does espionage have to do with building or protecting an unshakable lifestyle? Plenty. What we'll discover is that solid ground can only be found in our most important relationships if we avoid a major friendship killer called *slander,* a biblical term that reflects the same techniques one master spy can use against another.

David's challenge in Psalm 15:3 reads: "He does not slander with his tongue." Literally, the Hebrew reads, "He does not take up slander on his tongue."

That's a subtle but important difference as we begin to flesh out David's instructions here. Namely, what God has in mind is not incidental, accidental slips of the tongue but the purposeful act of "lifting up and placing on our tongue" words of slander.

Let me (John) illustrate this distinction. At times, even a loved one can say something unintentionally that can hurt our feelings. One day this past winter, I had just finished dressing for work and had come out to join the rest of the family for breakfast. I was wearing a new gray sweater that I thought looked particularly good. And apparently my older daughter, Kari, thought so, too. "Oh, Dad," she exclaimed when I rounded the corner into the kitchen, "that sweater looks great on you!"

Inside, I beamed as I thought, *Well, I* have *lost some weight . . . and it* was *a great buy . . . and Kari* does *have such good taste . . .*

The spell was broken when she added, "It's the same color as your hair!"

Now, I don't know about you, but I don't like to be reminded that I'm getting older. So my daughter's observation concerning my hair was the last thing I wanted to hear. But I'd call her comment an *inadvertent* insult, not slander. It was just a cute, little kid telling the truth about her graying dad. Her comment was made by accident, not by taking careful aim. Such an occasional slip of the tongue has nothing to do with the serious charge being leveled here. That's because slander was no laughing matter in David's day— nor is it in our own.

Behind the Word *Slander*

Today, twisting the truth has become so commonplace, we can go to any newsstand and read it in the headlines of the tabloids. Or we can turn on

CNN and hear character assassination as a routine part of political small talk. But to really understand what the Bible calls slander, we need to combine two incredibly negative words.

I Spy

The first meaning of the Hebrew word for *slander* is literally "to spy, to search out." For example, do you remember the dramatic scene in Genesis 42 when Joseph first met his brothers after they had tossed him into a pit and then sold him into slavery as a youth? As grown men, they had now come seeking food, but what they had unknowingly found was their younger brother—Pharaoh's appointed ruler over Egypt.

Though their eyes were blinded to who he was, Joseph instantly recognized his brothers and baited them with the words, "You are spies; you have come to look at the undefended parts of our land" (Gen. 42:9).

"Oh no!" they cried.

But Joseph cut them short with this challenge: "It is as I said to you; you are spies . . . !" (Gen. 42:14). Literally, what Joseph said to his brothers could be translated, "You are slanderers!" He was accusing them of something Moses and Joshua actually did when they sent out groups of spies before going to war.

In other words, when someone commits what the Bible calls slander, he or she is engaging in an age-old practice of searching out another's weaknesses. For most spies, that involves getting as close as they can to an enemy, learning his knowledge, gaining his trust, even sharing his table . . . and all the while having a destructive ulterior motive.

Slander is gathering inside information on a friend or loved one and twisting it with others in order to do the person serious harm.

That aspect of slander is linked with an equally negative partner. Listen to two graphic word pictures behind a second way the word is translated: "Like a leopard I will lie in wait by the wayside. I will encounter them like a bear robbed of her cubs, and I will *tear open* their chests" (Hosea 13:7-8) and "Then the king arose, *tore his clothes . . .* " (2 Sam. 13:31, emphases added).

Thus, this second meaning of slander is "to rip, tear, or rend." Put the two together and what do you get? Not a Disney jingle, but an accurate picture of the destructive power of slander. Slander is gathering inside information on a co-worker, friend, or loved one and twisting it with others in order to do the person serious harm.

"I'd never do that!" you might say. But don't be too quick to chalk up this lifestyle trait in the "That's One Sin I Regularly Skip" category. For unfortunately, slander is one of the most common Christian practices today. That's because even though it can leave serious scars on the one it hits, it's rarely traceable to the one who fired the shot. Just ask Pastor Mike.

Hidden Fury

Diane didn't look like a murderer. She was a PTA mom, a Sunday school teacher, and a regular part of a weekly women's Bible study. But though she might have thought her words were insignificant, they set off a firestorm that killed a man's promising career and proved the words of Proverbs 18:21: "Death and life are in the power of the tongue."

Her simply "helpful" action reminds us of a best-selling book called *The Gun.* It's a story that traces a murder weapon back to crime after crime, from the first day it was purchased. The point was to show how many predatory hands that one gun went through on its deadly path toward murder.

If you traced back the "smoking gun" that destroyed Mike's pastoral career and nearly ended his marriage, it began with Diane's picking up a destructive weapon called slander and squeezing the trigger. It happened one day when she was very angry. If she was honest about it, she'd have to admit that there was just a touch of revenge prompting her when she picked up the phone and dropped that first hint.

After all, she needed that part-time job. She was qualified for it. It fit her and the kids' schedules perfectly. And if Mike, that "arrogant" new children's pastor, hadn't filled it with a college student instead of a married woman, for heaven's sake, she'd have been the new preschool coordinator!

It wasn't as if she didn't have genuine grounds for her suspicions, after all. She had been late to church that Sunday, and she was walking by his office when she saw him through the space in his not-quite-closed curtains—in there all alone with one of his young students, Becky Stewart, and the door was shut. Sure, it was Sunday morning, and sure, she didn't see anything alarming. But it was unusual . . . *highly unusual* . . . for a male teacher to be alone with a female student like that.

She'd meant to make just that one call to Becky's mother. But she wasn't home. So Dianne had *had* to call another friend for "counsel" on what to do about this situation . . . which was upgraded to a problem after her second call . . . which mushroomed into a crisis with a third call.

When Diane finally got Becky's mother on the phone (after two more "necessary" calls), she was now fully convinced it was her responsibility to expose the "truth" of what *could have been* a scene of improper conduct.

In near panic, Becky's mom dropped the phone and ran to her daughter's room, demanding to know if Pastor Mike had done anything to her that past Sunday. Shocked and misunderstanding what her mother meant, Becky nodded her head and admitted that he had "made her feel uncomfortable" when she was in his office.

That was all it took to turn a spark into an explosion.

What Becky didn't say that afternoon was the reason for her discomfort. Pastor Mike had brought her into his office to talk about her deliberately pushing down another girl on the playground—for the second time. Instead of correcting her in front of the other children and teachers, Pastor Mike had walked her into his office to talk about what Jesus would do to make things right.

Had Mike shown poor judgment? Yes. Was he a raving pedophile turned loose on the church? Absolutely not. But by the time Becky's father got the message and rushed home, the phone lines had burned up from the uncounted calls made between "concerned" church members, and both the senior pastor *and* Child Protective Services (CPS) had been called . . . and *still* no one had talked directly to Pastor Mike.

Remember our definition of slander? It was "gathering inside information on a friend or loved one and twisting it with others in order to do the person serious harm." We'd say Diane's "helpful" words fit like a glove.

You can imagine the rest of the story. Mike was placed on temporary leave until things could be sorted out, which in his case never happened. Even though he was finally exonerated of all charges and accusations, at one point in the process CPS threatened to take his own children away. And in the weeks that followed, the fallout and suspicious looks from once-friendly parishioners pushed up the pressure so much that his wife and his marriage nearly fell apart.

Mike works days now at a hotel, checking in travelers instead of checking on Sunday school supplies. What started as a single act of slander ended up like a feather pillow ripped open on a windy day, leaving Mike to pick up the scattered feathers of his reputation.

Please don't get us wrong. There are people, even pastors, who take illegal and terrible advantage of children at church. Between the two of us, we have three daughters, so don't think we don't err on the side of caution when a young child is involved. But the error Diane made in launching purposely slanderous calls wasn't prompted by a heightened concern for Becky Stewart, but by a clear desire to harm Pastor Mike. And the result of her peeking through a window and drawing erroneous conclusions was that a good man and his family nearly went down in smoke.

Parting Applications

Let's close our look at this admonition against slandering by making three everyday applications.

1. Realize that the closer we get, the more wrinkles we'll see.

As we begin this section on protecting our most important relationships, keep something in mind: The closer we get to someone, the more we'll see the person's faults, foibles, and weaknesses. So, as we see that roommate, workmate, loved one, or friend in a closer light, we need to remember Christ's words to take the log out of our own eyes before we complain about the splinter in someone else's (see Matt. 7:3-5). We also need to think of 1 Corinthians 13, where the kind of love is described that asks first, "How can I help the person grow in this area?" not "How can I use this against him or her?"

2. Understand that pointing the finger of slander at others points three fingers back at ourselves.

Have you ever been at the water cooler or in the lunchroom when someone began ripping apart a boss or co-worker? Like gossip, slander can spread like wildfire through a workplace . . . but it often leaves a trail pointing right to the spark that ignited it. We need to realize that when people hear us slandering others, they assume we'll say derogatory things about *them* when they're not around. And who wants to be around someone you can't trust?

We may think we're getting back at someone by spreading slanderous accusations about him or her, and sometimes our intent to harm does cause injury. But it always damages our character and witness and leaves us on shaky, not solid, ground with our co-workers, family, and friends.

3. Instead of lifting up slander, try carrying around encouraging words.

I don't remember the night my (John's) father called home to tell my mother he wasn't coming back. I didn't notice her tears or see her wondering what a displaced homemaker did. After all, I was only two months old, and this was long before there were any displaced-homemaker programs she could attend.

The year was 1952 when my mother suddenly became single. She had three boys, all under age three, to raise. No job. No degree. No relatives or large bank accounts to draw on.

I didn't hear her cry herself to sleep that night. But as the days and years unfolded, I came to understand a crucial decision she'd made soon after that fateful day. Namely, with God's help, she would build a home with as much love and security as she could. And she made another decision in those early days as well. No matter what, she would spend her time building up her children, not tearing down their father.

As I was to learn in later years from others, my mother could have taken shot after shot at my father, from his unfaithfulness to his failure to ever once make a child-support payment. Yet she was wise enough to know that dishonoring him wouldn't build anything positive in our lives. She wasn't untruthful or a Pollyanna. She simply felt her time was better spent encouraging us boys rather than filling our hearts with anger toward our father.

As we get close to others, why not use our inside information for good, not evil? To build up, not break down? To encourage, not enrage? Avoiding the relationship killer of slander can help strengthen the foundations of our families, friendships, and working relationships—and point us toward God's rock-solid ground.

 *Reflections*
Avoiding Interpersonal Espionage

1. It has been said that we often treat our friends better than our families. Have you found that to be true or false in your life? Why?

2. Think of a time when you were the victim of an inadvertent insult such as John's story about his gray hair that matched his sweater. How did you feel when that happened? How did you respond to the person?

3. How well do you know the weaknesses of your family members? Work associates? Do you view their weaknesses as something to protect or to exploit? How have you protected or exploited them?

4. Reread the story of Diane and Pastor Mike. If she had approached you with the information about Mike, how would you have responded? If she asked your advice on how to proceed, what would you have told her?

5. Reread the three applications at the end of the chapter. How can you put them into practice this week?

6. Read Proverbs 19:11. How does that verse relate to the subject of slander, and especially to the story of Diane and Pastor Mike? How might you use that verse in your life?

7. If you wandered down to the water cooler at work and heard two people slandering the boss, how might you change the subject to one of encouragement?

Chapter 12

THE FIFTH KEY

Refusing to Lend a Harmful Hand

Nor does evil to his neighbor . . .

When we think of someone "doing evil" to others, names come to mind like Capone, Manson, Bundy, and Dahmer. Then there are the lesser-known names that fill our newspapers almost every day—like Abrahams.

One afternoon in 1984, "Mo" Abrahams took a 30-pound mallet to the front yard of his home. Then, right before his 12-year-old son, he calmly beat his wife, Virginia, to death. She had just filed for divorce, alleging years of physical, mental, and sexual abuse.

Did he pay for this crime on death row or with 100 years in prison? *With our criminal justice system?* Guess again. In fact, Abrahams has even used his time behind bars to make a profit. In 1986, he was sentenced to life in prison, but including time spent waiting to be sentenced, he'll be eligible for parole in 1999. And when he walks away from jail in a few years, he'll even have a cash bonus waiting for him. That's thanks to the help he has received in prison from his union, the Michigan Education Association.

It seems that before he murdered his wife, Abrahams had been dismissed from an Ann Arbor school after five students testified he had made improper advances toward them. Abrahams appealed, and in 1986, *while he was in prison,* his case came before the State Tenure Commission.

Amazingly, on a 2-2 vote, the commissioners held for Abrahams. (One of the commissioners who voted to pay Abrahams was himself convicted of sexually assaulting a 14-year-old boy a year later and is now serving time in prison.) They awarded him back pay, *plus* raises, *plus interest* from the time he was fired in 1980 until the day he killed his wife. A tidy nest egg is now just waiting for him the day he steps through those prison doors.

When we speak of something as evil today, it usually has to be in the unusual, outrageous, or even shocking category to warrant the label—heartless child killers like those who set off the bomb in Oklahoma City; coldblooded car-jackers hunting down German tourists; drug dealers killing a family of seven in which the youngest child was only three; or emboldened crooks walking into a Washington, D.C., police station and killing five officers and FBI agents.

That's evil . . . right? Right. No question about it. But before you turn to the next chapter, we need to take a look at what God's Word says about this action we're commanded to avoid in Psalm 15:3. For in Scripture, *evil* carries an everyday level of conviction that may surprise you.

There's More to Doing Evil Than Committing Murder

When the Bible defines the word *evil,* among its many occurrences are two pictures that help to illustrate its meaning. One picture concerns a miracle the prophet Elisha performed after taking over for his mentor, Elijah. The men of Jericho came to him with an urgent request. "Behold now, the situation of this city is pleasant, as my lord sees; but the water is bad, and the land is unfruitful," they said (2 Kings 2:19).

What was wrong with the water? It was bitter, polluted, sickening to the taste. Literally, the Bible says the water was "evil."

In response, Elisha threw a jar of salt into the water, and we're told, "So the waters have been purified to this day, according to the word of Elisha which he spoke" (2 Kings 2:22).

One picture of evil, then, is of something that's polluted. A second adds another graphic image. In Jeremiah 24, God gave the prophet Jeremiah a vision he was to communicate to the nation. The Lord showed Jeremiah two baskets of figs and then asked, "What do you see, Jeremiah?"

"Figs, the good figs, very good; and the bad figs, very bad, which cannot be eaten due to rottenness" (Jer. 24:3). Literally, they couldn't be eaten due to their being "evil."

Do you begin to see a clearer picture of what doing evil to a neighbor entails? It's not just ending his or her life. It's also doing something that "muddies the water" for the person or "spoils" the good that could or should come his or her way—just like what Henry did to his former friend with a letter.

Paying Back Good for Evil

Henry wasn't just looking for a job when Steve hired him—he was desperate. And even though he didn't have all the qualifications Steve would have preferred, Steve saw something in the young man he liked. He offered Henry a job, including paying him for the time he spent training on the business's computer.

Henry was to be the director of communications for an up-and-coming tennis club in a nice location in their city. Steve was the general manager and a committed Christian. And in the months to come, he would share his faith and continue to encourage Henry in many ways.

A year after Henry was hired, the club's board of directors held its annual meeting. The local economy had taken a turn for the worse, and new memberships were down. In a cost-cutting move, the board voted over Steve's objection to "downsize just in case," and three staff positions were eliminated . . . including Henry's.

Steve had the hard task of telling all three employees that their positions no longer existed. But at least he felt good about the three months' severance package he had won from the board, and he felt his offer to write a glowing letter of recommendation for each of them showed his level of appreciation and understanding.

That's not what Henry saw, however. He was furious over being "canned" by the board, and he felt sure the decision was Steve's doing. Even as he listened to Steve's offer of severance and appreciation for his efforts, Henry determined in his mind to get "payback." And as he thought, he realized he'd been trained in just the means to do it.

Steve had graciously given Henry the rest of the day off to go and talk to his wife or begin to look for another job. All he asked was that Henry come in the next morning, clean out his office, turn in his keys, and then pick up his severance check. But that gave Henry the opportunity to come in that night, after the club was closed, and "fix" Steve and the computer system.

Henry first copied onto his own floppy disk the club's complete mailing list, and then he sabotaged the main computer that held the club's important financial data. Although Steve could never prove that Henry had damaged the data on their computer, Steve soon experienced his ex-employee's anger in a second, scathing way—an unsigned letter that went to each member, filled with lies and inaccuracies, accusing Steve of skimming money from the club and of treating employees in an unethical and immoral way.

In a special meeting, the directors gave Steve their full vote of confidence and issued their own letter in response. But that didn't stop Henry's letter from muddying the waters—from polluting the good feelings many club members had felt toward Steve and bringing his hard-won reputation into question.

> **God hates evil because, when we seek to muddy, pollute, or destroy another person's life, family, or business, we're tapping into a long line of evil.**

From a biblical perspective, evil is more than just physically harming a person. It's something despised by God. The apostle Peter wrote, "For the eyes of the LORD are upon the righteous, and His ears attend to their prayer, *but the face of the LORD is against those who do evil*" (1 Pet. 3:12, emphasis added).

There's plenty of reason for God to hate evil. In part it's because when we seek to muddy, pollute, or destroy another person's life, family, or business, we're tapping into a long line of evil. Listen to these pointed words in 1 John: "By this the children of God and the children of the devil are obvious: anyone who does not practice righteousness is not of God. . . . For this is the message which you have heard from the beginning, that we should love one another; not as Cain, who was of the evil one, and slew his brother" (1 John 3:10–12*a*).

Can you see now why God is so adamant about evil being sinking sand? Like Cain, when we do evil to another person, we're reflecting character traits from Satan's family line, not God's. That's why John would implore the church later, saying, "Beloved, do not imitate what is evil, but what is good. The one who does good is of God; the one who does evil has not seen God" (3 John 11).

Doing evil is no minor folly to be easily excused or quickly written off, particularly when it's practiced in one of our most important relationships—like that with a close neighbor.

A Neighbor Close at Hand . . .

When David gave us this fifth step toward solid ground, he put an added word on the end. We're not to do evil to our "neighbor." In Old Testament times, there was much to be said for a neighbor. In fact, in the Book of Proverbs, we're told, "Better is a neighbor who is near than a brother far away" (Prov. 27:10).

Better than a brother? Old Ed down the street, who won't return my mower?

If you could have asked those on our American frontier if they'd rather have a neighbor close by whom they could count on to help fight off hostiles or put up a barn—or a brother living safely in Poughkeepsie—they would have chosen the neighbor every time. Nothing against family relationships, but on the frontier, the day-to-day ability of a neighbor to be a source of encouragement and help outweighed even the fruitcake sent by a sister far away.

And therein lies a key to anchoring our character in solid ground. Namely, with those we see regularly, we're to do good, not evil. You know who we mean—the people across the street whom we see at their best at a Christmas party or at their worst picking up the morning newspaper; those neighbors in the next cubicle or office who occasionally talk too loud or leave the popcorn in the microwave too long; that family next door that seemed so understanding when our daughter's girlfriends "papered" their house by mistake, but get so annoyed when our dog chooses their yard as his favorite spot.

Though they're not precluded by the term *neighbor,* nameless strangers aren't really in view here—the people who pull in front of us when we drive, wait to fill out their deposit slips when we're behind them in line at the bank, or wear their cowboy hats and pick the seat in front of us at the movies. Instead, the reference is to close neighbors and friends God has put us in contact with nearly every day. Such people should be daily recipients of the first three elements of Psalm 15—integrity, righteousness, and truth—not of the killers of close relationships—evil turns, rotten tricks, and dirty words.

But again, unless we're a Sunday school teacher by day and a cat burglar or drug dealer by night, it's so hard to look at ourselves as evil. Evil is for urban gangs like the Crips and Bloods. For hoods and hooligans. For riffraff and renegades. It's not for churchgoers who vote in every election and pay their full share (and more) of local, state, and federal taxes.

"I'm not evil!" you might say. And we're sure you're not. But let's take a look at five less-obvious aspects of evil—five actions that we need to make sure don't show up on our neighbors' doorsteps or in our loved ones' laps.

Five "Low-Flying" Aspects of Evil

One reason our war birds put such a dent in the fully alerted air defenses of Iraq during Operation Desert Storm had to do with altitude. Namely, the first wave of stealth attack bombers that came into Baghdad flew at literal treetop level—below radar detection—before hitting their targets.

What works for warplanes also works for evil. For though there are obvious actions of hate, violence, and injustice that clearly show up on our "radar" screens, there are several aspects of evil that can scream in below our normal threat detectors and harm people nonetheless.

Like what? Like the five reflections of evil that follow.

1. Evil people refuse to acknowledge or admit their own sinfulness.

Do you know someone who refuses to admit when he or she is wrong? Who doesn't just struggle to say "I'm sorry" but *never* says it? Or who is quick to deny any fault or weakness in his or her life?

It's like the story of the two sisters who got into a big fight one Thanksgiving over whose pumpkin pie was better. Angry words were exchanged, and as a result of the spoiled holiday, not another word was spoken between the two of them for more than 20 years. Finally, one sister fell deathly ill. Urged by family members, the other sister drove to her dying sister's hometown and walked into her hospital room.

"Martha," she said, "I'm sorry."

"Emily," her sister said in a feeble, halting voice, "I'm sorry, too, and I forgive you. But if I get better, things stay the way they were!"

It took a deathbed to get those sisters to admit they were wrong. With some people who practice evil, however, even that doesn't convict them. It's a biblical basic that we admit when we're wrong. The apostle John put it this way: "If we confess our sins, He is faithful and righteous to forgive us our sins and to cleanse us from all unrighteousness. If we say that we have not sinned, we make Him a liar, and His word is not in us" (1 John 1:9–10). It may not seem at first glance that an unrepentant spirit is an act of evil, but it is.

2. Evil people attack others instead of facing their own failures.

Not only will evil people resist admitting their sins and faults, but they'll turn on anyone who confronts them. The Book of Proverbs puts it this way: "Do not reprove a scoffer, lest he hate you; reprove a wise man, and he will love you" (Prov. 9:8).

As a senior associate pastor, Don learned this lesson in wise living the hard way when he pointed out a problem he saw in his senior pastor's life. Don prayed hard about talking with him. He searched his own eye to remove any "log" there before bringing up a "speck" in his boss's. But the extra time and attention the senior pastor seemed to spend on one secretary was causing several of the staff to talk.

Don felt that one aspect of his job was to help protect his pastor's reputation, so he quietly and in private brought out his concerns. In response, the pastor loudly and publicly denounced him and demanded his resignation for "disloyalty." Don was ushered out of the church unceremoniously and in shock. But three years later, it was an even greater shock to the church body and the community when this same senior pastor was caught in the act.

Scripture tells us that evil people dwell in darkness, not light. It's hard to have someone turn up the lights on a weakness, bad attitude, or compromising action in our lives. And at times, you'll run into a critical person who enjoys hurting others with words or charges that are unwarranted and even dead wrong. But some people won't accept any criticism. And if you do confront them, they buck and kick like a rodeo bronc just let out of the chute. These are people whom Shakespeare's oft-quoted words seem to fit when they're challenged: "I fear thou dost protest too much." Those who turn and attack others as evil for pointing out their faults are often hiding or projecting evil onto their confronter.

Keep in mind that with feet of clay, we're all going to be defensive at times. None of us likes to be wrong or have it pointed out. But dramatic defensiveness should not become a habit.

3. Evil people spend great effort maintaining the appearance of purity.

It's clear in Scripture that even though he was the king of Israel for a time, Saul carried evil in his heart. It's not just that Saul hired a witch to foretell his future (a horoscope that really became a horror-scope as he saw his upcoming death); he also put substance over reality in his worship of God and in his walk before God's people. Let us explain.

It might be hard for us to understand now, but at the time, God directly commanded Saul to be the agent of extermination for a king named Agag and all his people (see 1 Sam. 15). From practicing divination and child sacrifice to opposing God's people as they were in great need coming out of Egypt, the Amalekites had earned God's wrath, and Israel's army was to be His instrument of judgment. Yet Saul didn't follow through on God's clear words. Instead of destroying all the Amalekites and their possessions, "Saul and the people spared Agag and the best of the sheep, the oxen, the fatlings, the lambs, and all that was good, and were not willing to destroy them utterly; but everything despised and worthless, that they utterly destroyed" (1 Sam. 15:9).

As you can imagine, Almighty God was not pleased. And He sent Samuel, His prophet, to confront Saul. When faced with his sin, Saul denied it at first; then he countered by blaming it on the "people." Yet Samuel cut him to the quick with the words, "Has the LORD as much delight in burnt offerings and sacrifices, as in obeying the voice of the LORD? . . . Because you have rejected the word of the LORD, He has also rejected you from being king" (1 Sam. 15:22-23).

That got Saul's attention. If he wasn't king . . . there wouldn't be a kingdom to rule. And with that thought, out came a quick, compromised confession. "I have sinned," Saul said. "I have indeed transgressed the command of the LORD . . . , because I feared the people and listened to their voice" (1 Sam. 15:24).

When Samuel stood firm in refusing to reinstate him and turned to go, Saul grabbed his robe, ripping it. It was a picture of God's ripping the kingdom from Saul's hands that day.

Close to begging, Saul issued another apology to Samuel. But watch closely what came from his amazingly uncontrite heart. Saul knew that if Samuel walked away from him, it would become public knowledge that he had fallen from God's grace. So he pleaded with Samuel to keep up his image: "'Please honor me now before the elders of my people and before Israel, and go back with me, that I may worship the LORD your God.' So Samuel went back following Saul, and Saul worshiped the LORD" (1 Sam. 15:30–31).

Evil people like Saul can use even a time of confession to engage in image management. Saul wasn't really cut to the heart. He was covering his tracks.

When the people saw him arm in arm with Samuel, he would still have the appearance of purity . . . despite having a depraved heart.

In recent years, we've seen certain TV evangelists who have used their fall into sin as a platform for public repentance. But in one notable case, the man's quick confession was just a cover-up before another, much-publicized slip into sin. What he and others like him today seek to do, like Saul before them, is to maintain an image, not a life based on truth. And that's a sure recipe for sinking, not solid, ground.

4. Evil people seek to squash growth in others, not encourage it.

Mandy stayed after the Young Life club meeting I (John) led and talked at length with one of the girl leaders. Finally, I was called over to talk with them, and in the process I first heard a family story of evil. Mandy was a young lady with incredible, God-given musical talents. She was also the object of squashing control of her gifts by her parents.

In early grade school, Mandy had been allowed by her teachers to play the piano before and after school. Even without formal lessons, she excelled. She could quickly pick up tunes by ear, and she transferred that same talent to the clarinet and the school band when she was old enough. She was so good that she was asked to play in the concert band as a freshman in high school—but her parents said no. She was asked to play in the school orchestra her sophomore year, and again they said no. Later she was encouraged to apply for a music scholarship for college, whereupon she received an absolute and definitive no from her parents.

When her music teacher called and talked with her parents after that last denial, they insisted they knew what was best for their daughter, and college and music weren't it.

As the three of us talked that night after the Young Life meeting, it turned out that it wasn't just music her parents said no to. It was also dating, getting her driver's license, spending the night at a friend's house, going to a youth camp, or anything else that looked remotely like a growth opportunity for Mandy.

In tears, Mandy asked for help. So I called and went by to talk with her parents myself. They were nice enough people when we sat down. But I soon became uneasy, and within a few minutes, I wept inside for what Mandy faced daily. Never before had I sensed so much control used so defiantly to crush and destroy. Unfortunately, in counseling sessions I've seen it many times since. In fact, after my visit to Mandy's home, her parents said an absolute no to one more thing in her life . . . going to Young Life.

Though their actions shocked me at the time, today I understand much better what motivated them. That's because I've seen more of the effects of evil, and evil always seeks to destroy. In fact, one name for Satan in Scripture is "destroyer." And a hurtfully controlling spouse, parent, child, boss, or friend is simply reflecting the evil of that destructive line. If love and truth free a person (remember the verses "You shall know the truth, and the truth shall make you free" [John 8:32] and "For God so loved the world . . ." [John 3:16]), evil enslaves.

Mandy lived with an out-of-control controller. (And if you work with, live with, or know one, we heartily recommend our good friend Dr. Tim Kimmel's book *How to Deal with Powerful Personalities*.) Yet Jesus said clearly that we're not to be like the Gentiles and "lord it over" those we live or work with. Rather, if we're committed to dwelling on God's solid ground, we should be helping people grow and be giving them the freedom to do so.

5. Evil people demand love while denying responsibility.

A best-selling book from several years ago was called *Passive Men and Wild Women*. It unerringly describes the malady affecting many couples we see in counseling, and it points out how damaging a state of imbalance in a home can be. As an example, you may have a man who is forceful at work but becomes passive, uninvolved, and unwilling to aid in decisions and even basic maintenance of the home. As a result, the wife becomes frustrated, angry, and verbal about her displeasure.

That leads to the man becoming even more passive by hiding in front of the television, tuning her out, or staying at work (or a combination of all three). That causes the woman to have to take on even more responsibilities around the house and at work . . . and to actively resent it more and more. Soon you've got one person who is majoring in passivity, while the other is having an internal nuclear reaction.

Can you see anything wrong with this picture? Can you see anything evil?

It isn't just Rush Limbaugh, Ken Hamblin, and Laura Schlessinger who make daily calls for the people in our nation to "take responsibility" and move away from a welfare state. God has always called His people to a life of responsibility. "Husbands, love your wives" (Eph. 5:25). "Wives, be subject to your own husbands" (Eph. 5:22). "Children, obey your parents" (Eph. 6:1). "Let every person be in subjection to the governing authorities" (Rom. 13:1).

It's not just wrong for us to deny our basic responsibilities to our spouses and families—it's evil. That's why Paul was so condemning when he said that the one who doesn't provide for his family is "worse than an infidel" (1 Tim. 5:8).

Five reflections of evil—from refusing to see our sins to reneging on our clear responsibilities (and in-between, attacking those who lovingly confront us, maintaining the appearance of purity without its substance, and squashing growth opportunities in those we seek to control). None of these may make headline news, but they can just as easily kill a close relationship as any murderer who shows up on television.

We've seen how godly men and women who want their lives built on the Rock will settle on the solid ground of integrity, righteousness, and truth. We've also seen how these same people will actively avoid any opportunity to slander or do evil to a neighbor. Now we need to consider the third thing David listed as sinking sand that we need to avoid. It's the sixth key to anchoring our lives on biblical bedrock, and it cautions us to never take part in an unholy harvest.

 **Reflections**

Refusing to Lend a Harmful Hand

1. How do you define the word *evil?* What examples can you give to reinforce that definition?

2. John and Rick referred to the proverb "Better is a neighbor close at hand than a brother far away." When have you found that to be true in your experience? How could you prove to be a close neighbor this week?

3. John and Rick listed five "low-flying" aspects of evil. Which of them is the greatest struggle for you? Why?

4. How hard or easy is it for you to say the words "I was wrong. Will you forgive me?" How would your husband/wife/children/co-workers answer that same question? Why not ask them and see if your answers match?

5. How do you respond when confronted with something you've done wrong? (Circle your answer.)

   Attack   Protest   Debate   Listen   Consider   Agree   Change

6. Rate yourself on the following scale on how important other people's opinions are to you.

   Little or no effect   *Extremely important*

   1   2   3   4   5   6   7   8   9   10

   How does this influence what you do or how you approach certain actions or decisions?

7. Do you understand the biblical expectations for your behavior? How well are you fulfilling them? How does your current level of effort and progress compare to last year's effort and progress?

Chapter 13

The Sixth Key

Not Adding Insult or Injury

Nor takes up a reproach against his friend . . .

arah Randall was at the top of her world. She had breezed through her undergraduate work, earning a reputation for clear, careful thinking; an innovative approach to problem solving; as well as an ability to express the results of her study in concise, understandable reports. After graduation, she pursued her master's degree, earning it in just over a year. Before beginning on her doctorate, she landed an entry-level job as a research assistant at another major university. There she had won the admiration and respect of her peers and the applause of her professors.

She worked on a team with one of the leading researchers in her field. The team he had built was pioneering a new method of handling one of the department's thorniest problems—one that had plagued their research for months. It was challenging, exhausting, disheartening, and thrilling. She wouldn't have traded a moment of it for anything in the world.

One morning, while working on her own, Sarah stumbled across something that showed promise in providing the needed key to unlock the problem. With each step in her exploration, it became clearer she had discovered what so many had been seeking for so long. Following through on her reputation for thorough, careful research, she tested and retested her theory and triple-checked the results. By 2:00 the next morning, there was no doubt in her mind. She'd found the answer.

She hurried back to her apartment for a few hours' sleep, quickly showered, dressed, inhaled her breakfast, and was back at the lab by 7:30 to show the results to her boss when he came in at 8:00. Excitement and anticipation were written all over her face—she couldn't wait to hear his praise and see his smile.

That excitement quickly eroded when his response to her data was little more than a shrug and a "That's interesting." She was sure there would have been at least a departmental meeting, with an opportunity to share what she had found with her colleagues. Instead, he mentioned how the "best people in his department" had been tracking down false leads for months and how he'd have one of "them" look at what she'd done. Then her data file was tossed in a basket on her boss's desk, along with a mountain of other memos and file folders.

Fatigued from the last 36 hours, Sarah took the rest of the day off, trying to lose herself in a good book and the warm sunshine of her patio, only to have her thoughts drift again and again to her boss's discouraging lack of excitement.

As far as she knew, her report never did get reviewed. The next week, she was transferred to another research project. And in less than two months, Sarah's position in the lab was phased out for "lack of funding." She was asked to leave all her notes behind, and she found little encouragement in her co-workers' assurances that someone with her talent would have no problem landing work elsewhere.

Sarah did find another research position, however, and she also started into her doctoral program. It was then that she attended a national symposium lined with speakers and workshops in her field. Among the many talks she heard, the last was a presentation about what was new on the horizon in their field. The keynote speaker was her former boss. Those who spoke before him did little to hold her interest, but 30 seconds into his presentation, she was riveted to every word he said.

He was presenting the results of exciting new research that promised to be a major breakthrough in the field. With each sentence, Sarah grew more incredulous. She couldn't believe what she was hearing. He was presenting the results of *her* investigation! To make matters worse, he made it sound as if all the exciting findings were the result of *his* work.

By the time he'd finished, she didn't know whether to scream or cry. All that effort, all that time and energy—stolen right out from under her. She'd even been talked into leaving behind all her notes. She didn't have a single piece of paper that could prove she was the one who had come up with these results. All this was done by an "expert," a man she'd looked at as a world leader and potentially a mentor. Not knowing what to do, she ran out of the meeting, stumbled down the hallway, bolted through the doors of the rest room, and collapsed in tears. *How could he do that,* she wondered, *how* could *he?*

She knew one thing. She wasn't sure exactly how or when, but she was going to get even. *I didn't do all that work to be outdone by one man's ego,* she thought. *He'll get his.* From that moment on, she began to think about "payback" and ways to make him look bad.

What became of Sarah's commitment to revenge? On the outside, it meant that she took every chance to demean her former employer's character. Her rhetoric was acid, and her tone of voice when discussing the situation was vitriolic. Yet without a shred of proof, and in the face of his high standing in the scientific community, soon *she* was the one who looked sick and untruthful. The initial ripple of support she received when she presented her charges quickly disappeared. And though railing about the injustice she had suffered grew to be her obsession, it fast became a tiring, alienating bore even to her close friends.

On the inside, without realizing the trade-off, Sarah had made a damaging exchange. Light, clarity, and clear thinking began to be swapped for inner darkness and a loss of positive direction—a transaction Scripture clearly describes in 1 John 2:11: "But the one who hates his brother is in the darkness and walks in the darkness, and does not know where he is going because the darkness has blinded his eyes."

Revenge and Betrayal

We doubt there's anyone who will read this book who can't, in some way, relate to what Sarah experienced. Even if the closest you've ever come to a research lab is a Pepsi Challenge taste test, you know what it's like to be betrayed. All of us can relate to Sarah's disappointment, anger, and desire for revenge.

No doubt King David could, too. The account of his relationship with Saul in 1 Samuel is a graphic portrait of a man who understood better than most what it's like to be in someone's confidence one minute and betrayed in the next. Chosen by God as the next king of Israel, David was taken into Saul's household and given a place of honor. He gladly played his harp to soothe Saul's soul during long, troubled nights. He valiantly went out and fought Saul's battles, leading Israel to victory after victory on behalf of his king. His best friend was Saul's son, and he gratefully took one of Saul's daughters as his wife.

What thanks did David receive for all his efforts and contributions to Saul's family? A death sentence issued by Saul himself. Years of hiding in the wilderness. Countless attempts to make things right, only to have Saul turn again and try to destroy him. If there was ever a man who had a right to speak ill of another—to take up a reproach against his friend—David was the man. (For some great insight into that relationship, read 1 Samuel 16–31.)

But guess who had a clear message for those who would consider countering betrayal with reproach? That's right, King David. In Psalm 15, he made it clear that men and women of God aren't to retaliate with reproach. To understand more about what David meant by not taking up a reproach against a friend, let's look more closely at his key terms.

Growing a Friendship . . . Then Cutting It Down

Three words bear closer examination. The first is the Hebrew word translated "take up," and it means to lift up something negative, like a critical comment about someone else. It's the same word used in Numbers 21 of the bronze serpent, a symbol of evil that was lifted up on a tribal standard for everyone to see. In other words, David said we're not to take an active, purposeful part in waving a character flaw or failing of a friend in front of others.

A godly person doesn't go out of his or her way to draw attention to a chink in a friend's armor.

If David were writing that line of Psalm 15 today, he might say something like this: "He doesn't go out of his way to draw attention to a chink in his friend's armor." To do that would mean spotlighting someone else's faults, something God strongly cautions against in Romans 14: "Who are you to judge the servant of another? To his own master he stands or falls. . . . But you, why do you judge your brother? Or you again, why do you regard your brother with contempt? For we shall all stand before the judgment seat of God" (Rom. 14:4*a*,10).

That's hard *not* to do in this day and age, however. From athletics to business to personal relationships, the world's way of doing things is to find the other guy's weakness and exploit it. That's even easier when the other person is genuinely at fault, and that leads us to the second word we need to clearly understand: *reproach.*

The Hebrew "picture" behind *reproach* might seem a little confusing at first, until you stop and think about it. It's the idea of "harvesting." What does farming have to do with friendships? A lot.

Consider the case of Jayne and her best friend, Susan. They'd been friends since high school and were in each other's weddings. They'd struggled through pregnancies, diapers, and teething together, and now their kids were well into grade school.

That's when, with both of their husbands' full support, they went into business together. Before the opening day of their boutique, they had spent almost 20 years as loving friends—watching each other's kids, commiserating about each other's husbands, caring about each other's futures. But within the eight months it took for their business to fail, their friendship caught fire and crashed right along with their fledgling enterprise.

The venom from both Jayne and Susan matched that of the king cobra we mentioned in chapter 9. No holds were barred in discussing who was at fault. And both women would go out of their way to ax the other's character in public, avoid talking directly to each other (or let the kids do so), and refuse even to stay in the same store if the other walked in.

Did you notice what happened? First there was the growing of a friendship. Over time. Carefully watered. Blessed by the sun. But then instead of enjoying a glorious harvest in their later years, they saw the failure of their business act like a runaway combine, cutting their relationship to pieces like wheat in a field. What was left was unusable stubble and hurt feelings where fullness of heart and soul should have been.

Farmers know what it means to harvest. For corn or wheat, it means to "cut it down." And that's exactly the meaning behind the word here. Perhaps now you can see where we get our expression, "He's cutting me down!"

We've looked at the fact that we're not to actively "take up" a fault or use our knowledge of a friend to "cut down" that person in a reproach. But who, exactly, are we not to reproach?

That's explained by the word *friend.* Here in Psalm 15:3, it's an unusual word, having as its root meaning "to be near." In many places, it means one's relatives; yet it's used in a broad enough way that it could stand for anyone with whom we have regular contact—a close friend or even a work or school acquaintance. As one writer has pointed out, the morality of the Old Testament bound each person to refrain from this sin, no matter what the formal relationship.[1] The same holds true for us.

We've seen the pictures behind this idea of not "cutting down" someone close to us. We need to also take a look at the damage that results if we do.

Scorched Ground

Why is taking up a reproach against someone so damaging? First, *if the reproach is based on false information, damage to another person's character could result.* In previous chapters, we've given examples of how an untruthful statement can shorten a career. That's bad, but there's worse. Recently, it shortened a man's life.

In one of the most amazing stories to come out of the sordid world of daytime television, something happened that nearly tops them all. On the "Jenny Jones Show," Jenny was asking people to guess who their secret admirer was. One male guest had been led to believe his was one of several female acquaintances who had also been invited on the show. When his secret admirer was asked to stand, however, it turned out to be a homosexual male friend. The first man was so upset about what he had learned and the way it had been broadcast on national television that the next day, he shot dead his previously secret admirer.

That's obviously the most extreme form of retaliation imaginable for what was perceived as damage to a person's reputation. But if looks could kill, many people would mow down their former friends who have spread false information about them.

Second, *taking up a reproach against someone violates the spirit of grace that should mark our relationships.* Paul told the Ephesians, "Let no unwholesome word proceed from your mouth, but only such a word as is good for edification according to the need of the moment, that it may give *grace* to those who hear" (Eph. 4:29, emphasis added). Shining a spotlight on someone else's faults, even if they're genuine, does little to show them the grace of God.

I (John) failed to follow this principle several years ago in a church where I served as an intern. For a period of time, I had a supervisor there who seemed incredibly critical. Every week, we had an hourly review luncheon where he would enjoy his meal while I felt as if I were the one being cooked over the grill.

He would criticize me for coming in 20 minutes late in the morning (even if I'd stayed at the church until after 1:00 A.M. the night before, cleaning up after an event). He would say that I was holding the child-care workers hostage and not following written directives when I let out my adult Sunday school class at 11:50 instead of 11:45. He even spent one whole lunch telling me how important it was to be consistent in my handouts and not mix Roman numerals with capital letters.

I would sit there, nodding my head and clenching my fists under the table. My blood would boil, and I couldn't wait for the ordeal to be over. At night, I'd complain to Cindy about how unfairly I was being treated.

Then came the end of my internship, and I got to do my own written evaluation of my supervisor. I took great delight in listing the man's faults. If I had been forced to endure such treatment, perhaps my harsh words would spare future interns some measure of suffering. At least that was my "righteous rationalization" for cutting him down. But what moved my pen that day was the reproach I'd taken up against that man.

A few weeks later, I was called into the office of my school's placement director. As I sat there, he asked about my experience with my supervisor.

Shifting uncomfortably in my seat, I told him I had put it all in writing, and I thought my words clearly expressed my feelings.

"I read your report, John," he said, "but it confuses me a little."

"How's that?" I said, thinking I had been quite clear about how demeaning and abrasive the man had been. Surely I wasn't the first intern who had written such a report about him.

"Well, John," the director said, "when your supervisor turned in his report on you, he wrote one of the most glowing evaluations we've ever received. He said he felt he had needed to be hard on you because you have so much potential. And from his comments, I'm sure he isn't aware of your harsh feelings toward him. I think you two need to talk."

The last thing I wanted to do was to talk to that man again. I thought that by venting my caustic feelings on that form, I had closed the door on a bad experience. But now, when confronted with my words, I saw them for what they really were. I hadn't made helpful comments but character slams that didn't reflect God's grace. I wasn't looking at why he had been so hard on me, nor had I considered the responsibility I had to talk with him if his critiques were upsetting me so much.

My writing had been prompted in part by a desire to teach him a lesson about "mistreating" interns. But actually, to my shame, *I* was the one who had much to learn. I did go and talk with that man, and I asked his forgiveness. I'm honored to say we're still good friends today . . . and I'm nearly world famous for ending my messages at conferences and churches *right on time.* These good things, however, happened only after I learned the hard way that taking up a reproach against someone can come back to haunt you and can hurt others as well.

Third, *taking up a reproach can sell short another person's potential for God.* All too often, we want to give up on a person because of a flaw we see in his or her character. When we highlight that to others, we run the risk of making that person's future for God less than it could be.

When the apostle Paul began his first missionary journey, he was accompanied by a number of people, among whom were Barnabas and Mark. Toward the end of that trip, they came to a place called Pamphylia, where Mark decided to hang it up and go home. Paul and Barnabas concluded their journey at Antioch, where an important theological debate arose. They went to Jerusalem to consult with the elders and apostles there about God's perspective on the issue.

After resolving the problem, Paul and Barnabas returned to Antioch with a letter from the Jerusalem leaders that clarified their position. Then Paul and Barnabas decided to return to the churches they'd seen on their first journey. Barnabas wanted to take Mark along, but Paul didn't. It's reasonable to assume that Paul took up a reproach against Mark. Tempers were flaring, and emotions were on edge. In fact, Paul and Barnabas disagreed so sharply that they parted company, each going his separate way.

Years later, Paul would again comment on Mark. In 2 Timothy 4:11, he said to Timothy, "Only Luke is with me. Pick up Mark and bring him with you, for he is useful to me for service." Interesting, isn't it? He'd written off his young comrade before, figuring he didn't have the makings of a missionary. But Barnabas wisely realized God wasn't through with Mark. So Barnabas took him under his wing and nurtured him to the point where Paul felt he was valuable enough to ask for by name.

Fourth, *a reproach can cause family wounds that are deep and long lasting.* When Jacob stole the blessing from Esau (to whom it belonged by the normal rules of inheritance), Esau's response was one of great grief and deep anger. Genesis 27:41 reads, "So Esau bore a grudge against Jacob because of the blessing with which his father had blessed him; and Esau said to himself, 'The days of mourning for my father are near; then I will kill my brother Jacob.'" The following verse tells us Esau didn't just keep that to himself. Rebekah, their mother, got wind of what he was planning and sent Jacob away. There's no doubt that if Esau was mad enough to kill Jacob, he was mad enough to take up a reproach against him.

Twenty years passed before the two brothers saw each other again. In that time, Esau's heart had softened—so much so that when he saw his long-lost brother, he embraced and kissed him (see Gen. 33:4). We offer that as encouragement to anyone who has taken up a reproach against a family member. With Christ's help, such wounds don't have to be permanent.

Still, it's important to remember that taking up a reproach against someone often creates a cancer in the relationship that's no fun to deal with. And once you start a pattern of reproach, it can have consequences that quickly escalate.

How Reproach Resembles Cancer

My (John's) twin brother, Jeff, is a cancer doctor who directs the scientific program in perhaps the finest cancer genetics laboratory in the country at the National Institutes of Health. One day, I asked him for information for a friend who had a fast-growing cancer. Jeff explained that the problem with cancer cells isn't necessarily that they grow and divide any faster than other cells. What makes cancer cells so deadly is that they don't *stop* dividing. While other cells have special instructions in their DNA that tell them when to quit multiplying, cancer cells have lost or choose not to respond to such a mechanism. In other words, once the ball gets rolling, it's difficult to stop.

The same is true of relationships in which a reproach has been leveled. The negative feelings and ill will can keep growing and growing. There's virtually nothing—outside of humility and seeking forgiveness—that can stop or reverse the process.

With so much at stake, it's important to understand how we can guard against taking up a reproach against someone we know. And we'd like to suggest three ways.

Three Ways to Guard Against Reproach

First, as much as possible, *look at the situation from the other person's point of view.* That's easy to say but extremely hard to do.

I (John) remember how hurt I was, growing up in a single-parent home, at my dad's very apparent anger and indifference toward us. There were times before I was a Christian when I certainly did take up a reproach against him. And even after coming to know Christ, I struggled to overlook his weaknesses and not react in anger. Then I met my Uncle Max.

While my dad was next to silent when it came to his past, my uncle (actually great-uncle) gave me a window into my father's troubled story. He pulled back the curtains on my dad's childhood, and for the first time I actually began to feel compassion, not contempt, for him. I learned that he had experienced a tumultuous relationship with his own father and strife with his brothers, and then he had seen incredible horrors while serving his country in wartime.

It's a challenge to try to see things from the other person's point of view. And it doesn't mean we excuse or downplay blatant sin because the person was a victim in some way. But gaining compassion and understanding of what the individual has been through can be extremely helpful in steering us away from reproach.

Second, *keep in mind that "getting even" is God's business, not ours.* Paul's words to the Christians in Rome are just as relevant today as they were then: "Never pay back evil for evil to anyone. Respect what is right in the sight of all men. If possible, so far as it depends on you, be at peace with all men. Never take your own revenge, beloved, but leave room for the wrath of God; for it is written, 'Vengeance is mine, I will repay,' says the Lord" (Rom. 12:17–19).

Those are hard words that fly in the face of what many in our culture say should be the norm. After all, how many people would buy a ticket to see Rambo deliberately not get even? But in God's program, Rambo's approach doesn't wash. Men and women committed to Him can be assertive in standing for what's right, but they're wrong in tearing down another person or carrying a reproach.

Finally, *realize that a perfect example of not taking up a reproach is none other than Christ Himself.* Peter spoke of Him this way: "For you have been called for this purpose, since Christ also suffered for you, leaving you an example for you to follow in His steps, 'who committed no sin, nor was any deceit found in His mouth'; and while being reviled, He did not revile in return; while suffering, He uttered no threats, but kept entrusting Himself to Him who judges righteously" (1 Pet. 2:21–23).

Notice two things: First, Christ didn't strike back at His accusers, even though He had every right. If anyone in history has ever deserved the opportunity to take up a reproach against someone, He did. Rather than put the Jews in their place, however, He remained silent. "He was oppressed and He was afflicted, yet He did not open His mouth; like a lamb that is led to slaughter, and like a sheep that is silent before its shearers" (Isa. 53:7).

Yes, it's true Christ conversed with His accusers. But that was only to clarify who He was and to answer their questions. Despite ample opportunity, He refused to launch a verbal attack against them. And that's nothing short of remarkable.

With such a high standard of love, it's no wonder that trying to apply Psalm 15 apart from the power of God is futile. (Remember how we first have to answer David's two questions: "O Lord, who may abide in Thy tent? Who may dwell on Thy holy hill?")

Second, Christ was able to do that because He implicitly trusted God the Father. There was no question the Father would deal righteously and fairly with Him. That confidence enabled Him to hold His tongue when anyone else would have been all too willing to call down that legion of angels and make mincemeat of his accusers.

The Book of Hebrews calls Jesus Christ the Captain of our faith. That means He has lived the life of faith He asks us to live, and He's qualified to give us the help we need to be faithful. So, the next time you're tempted to take up a reproach against someone, remember He understands what that temptation is like. If you've had someone break a promise to you, batter your reputation, or leave you broken, He experienced even more.

In addition, He's willing to bear *our* reproach. Paul told the Romans, "For even Christ did not please Himself; but as it is written, 'The reproaches of those who reproached Thee fell upon Me'" (Rom. 15:3). It's amazing enough to realize He faced the Cross without reproaching those who sent Him there. But to become the *object* of the *Father's* reproach for things *we've* done wrong? Now, that's love of epic—eternal—proportions. No one else will ever approach that. So, is it too much to ask that we—in a far more limited way—follow suit in our relationships?

Turning Wrongs Around

Wes Colfax was as godless as he was wealthy. He came up through the ranks in his company the hard way, starting in the unair-conditioned shipping room during summers in high school. But from the moment he set foot in Westover Industries, his ambition for power, prestige, and money began to drive him all the way to the president's chair. Wes's god was his career and the amenities of life it afforded him. No one was going to take that away.

His obsessiveness for the best even extended to his yard. Compulsive about neatness and presenting a professional look in everything, he made sure his lawn was the envy of the neighborhood. An immaculate, terraced yard with perfectly pruned shrubs and trees set the stage for a breathtaking view of flower beds and fountains that painted his property in picture-book glory. But that's not to say he did any actual yard work himself. The joke around the local landscape companies was that the three toughest jobs in America were "Colfax's yardman, Colfax's yardman, and Colfax's yardman."

At the time, Jake Sanders at Sanders Lawn Service had lasted longer in Colfax's employ than any other gardener. Though he'd been threatened with losing the account more times than he could remember, he'd learned to let Wes's barbs slide, continue to do the best he could, and in so doing, hang on to his most lucrative account. One day his crew was finishing a particularly tough job. Jake surveyed their handiwork with satisfaction, knowing they'd worked hard and completed their task in good time. As they loaded their equipment, Jake noticed clouds gathering on the horizon. "It's a good thing we finished when we did, men," he said. "Looks like there's a storm coming."

Just as Jake was saying that, Wes Colfax was on a commuter flight making its final approach at the local airport. By the time he landed, gathered his luggage, and got to his car, the squall was striking in full force. With rain coming down in sheets, rush hour traffic was backed up for miles. When he finally pulled through the security gate to the neighborhood, he was tired, hungry, and in a particularly foul mood.

He went to bed angry that night, and he came unglued the next morning when he walked down his driveway to get the paper. Strewn all over his lawn were leaves, pine needles, and trash. Furious that the yard looked like a war zone, he stormed into the house, yelled for his wife to get his phone book, and almost tore the phone off the wall. Before the woman at the answering service could finish saying, "Sanders Lawn Service," her ears were burning with a string of angry charges and expletives. When she asked him to calm down and stop his abusive language or she'd hang up, he said fine. In clipped words, spoken in staccato and full of fury, he said, "Leave . . . this . . . message. Sanders . . . you're . . . fired. What's more, I'll do everything I can to discourage everyone I know from ever using your pitiful service. You . . . got . . . that?"

She had. And Jake got the message when he arrived at his office.

Ten years went by. Jake's business survived despite the damage done by

Wes's accusations and vehement attempts to turn business away from him. More than once, Jake had to face caustic words or intense questions by a prospective client who had been poisoned by Wes.

But Jake was a world-class Christian, a Psalm 15 kind of person. He knew better than to eat up his own life by carrying a grudge against a bitterly unhappy man. Despite the temptation to reproach Wes's arrogance and immaturity, he stayed quiet and kept his nose to the grindstone. And God honored and blessed his business and family.

Wes, on the other hand, went through radical changes in his life. Driven to emotional and spiritual exhaustion by his obsession with money and power, he had a major heart attack. And in the incredible fear and confusion it brought, his pride and arrogance were finally broken. His cardiologist was an outstanding Christian who led his frightened friend to the comfort, freedom, and forgiveness of a relationship with Christ.

Wes's life changed from the minute he got out of the hospital. Like a modern Scrooge, he tried hard to start fresh and treat his family and others with respect. He also made his first attempt at attending church.

One morning, he decided to visit the church where his wife went, Covenant Bible Church. He walked in the door and was immediately impressed by the church's first-rate appearance. He made his way through the foyer and past a wall lined with pictures of missionaries serving all over the world. Then he made his way with the crowd into the sanctuary, where the usher at the door greeted him with a warm "hello" and handed him a bulletin.

That's when Wes's heart leaped into his throat. The usher was Jake Sanders.

Wes quickly shuffled past, trying to convince himself that there was no way Jake would remember. It had been 10 years! He nervously found his seat and quickly tried to lose himself in the details of the bulletin. But information about organ preludes and Saturday morning bake sales offered little distraction for a man haunted by a raging phone conversation years before.

As the service came to a close, Wes rose nervously from his seat and tried to sneak out the side door. But as he turned, there was Jake standing at the end of the aisle.

"Good morning again," Jake said. "My name is Jake Sanders. And I believe you're Wes Colfax, aren't you?"

Wes couldn't stand it any longer. Looking everywhere but at Jake, he tried to stammer his way through an apology. But no sooner had he begun his second sentence than Jake motioned for him to stop.

"Wes," Jake began, "no need to apologize. I understand."

"But you don't understand," Wes said. "I need to make this right. I'm a Christian now, and I need . . ." He swallowed hard. "I need to ask your forgiveness."

"You're forgiven," Jake said with a smile and an extended hand. "It's great to see you. *I've been praying for you for 10 years.*"

Wes couldn't believe it. Jake had every right to be angry and resentful for the heartache he'd put him through. But as Wes studied Jake's large frame and cheerful face, he saw no hint of what would be the typical human reaction . . . *reproach*. Jake didn't realize it then, but he'd won an admirer for life.

Jake gained some other things that day, too—a new friend, a Christian brother . . . and a new landscape contract for his son, who had taken over the business. Now Jake's son does Wes Colfax's yard—come rain or shine. And he always appreciates the warm greeting he gets and the liberal words of praise for a job well done.

Men like Jake know how important it is to choose not to take up a reproach against a friend. Instead, he took time he could have spent hating and prayed for a man previously entombed in his own greed and pride. You can rest assured that Wes Colfax has never forgotten Jake. And neither has his God.

If you want your life to settle on solid ground—ground more stable than anything the world can offer—be a person like Jake Sanders, who chose not to hold a grudge. Or like Corrie Ten Boom, a Holocaust survivor who, by God's grace, forgave one of her Nazi prison guards when he sought her out years later. Or like Elisabeth Elliot, who brought the gospel to the Indian tribe that had martyred her husband. All of them had plenty of reason to take up a reproach. Yet each chose to act like the Lord Jesus Christ—and they found a place of rock-solid rest as a result.

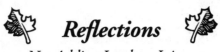

Reflections

Not Adding Insult or Injury

1. In what ways do people who want to get even typically retaliate?

2. Reread the story of Sarah Randall. If she continued to pursue her course of revenge, what might have happened to her? To her relationships?

3. Think of a time when you felt betrayed. How did you respond? If the same betrayal took place tomorrow, would you respond differently? Why or why not?

4. How do you feel when you see someone's "dirty laundry" paraded in public? Why?

5. John and Rick describe four ways in which taking up a reproach can hurt someone. Which one do you think causes the most pain to an individual? Why?

6. In your own words, how can looking at a situation from the other person's point of view affect our desire for revenge?

They Guide Our Public Walk

Chapter 14

THE SEVENTH KEY

Well-Placed Respect

In whose eyes a reprobate is despised, but who honors those who fear the Lord . . .

When I (Rick) was a college pastor several years ago, I had a group of students in a discipleship group. It just so happened we were studying Psalm 15. Each week, we'd focus on one of the 10 traits of a rock-solid lifestyle, then talk about how we could apply it. It was a group of motivated Christians, and my goal was to build godly character into each of those future leaders.

That's why what happened one night *after* our study hit me and my students so hard. After we had studied verse 4 on paper ("In whose eyes a reprobate is despised, but who honors those who fear the Lord"), God gave us an unexpected application of the passage on national television. Let me explain.

When the study was over that night, a few of the guys decided to hang around my house and watch TV. We turned the set on, and as we were surfing through the various channels, we came across a well-known "televangelist." As the TV preacher launched into his trademark theatrics, the guys in the room started cracking up and doing impersonations of him. Instead of correcting them, I joined in the fun. In fact, my imitation went a little overboard.

We all howled with laughter, sitting around the TV and ridiculing the man. But when he finished his message, he stopped and looked directly into the camera. "Before I leave you tonight," he said, "I have a message for some of you Christians out there who are watching."

Gradually, the chuckling stopped and the room grew quiet.

"I want to confront you right now," he said after a long pause. "If my preaching is wrong or I treat the Scriptures wrong, God will deal with me. But if you just don't like how I act or how I come across, *as Christians you have no right to make fun of me.*"

We all came to a dead stop. It was as if he were looking through the picture tube and right into my living room . . . staring at eight opened-mouthed believers. I had been the last one to do an impersonation of the man, and I felt like melting into the carpet. Here I was trying to be a role model and teach those college students how to develop godly character, and with my dishonoring imitation, God had used a television set to convict me!

We turned off the TV, then turned back to God's Word. And that night, we had an incredible discussion about what this verse really means and how easily we can belittle those of the faith.

Although I may not agree with the dramatics or the presentation of that particular evangelist, I do believe God used him that day to challenge me and those young men present. And He taught me some valuable lessons about the two words, *and the two worldviews,* presented in this seventh key to a rock-solid lifestyle: honoring those who deserve honor and viewing those who don't with reproach.

Understanding *Dishonor*

Clearly, what happened that night wasn't honoring to someone who fears the Lord. Yet, to understand just why that's so wrong, as well as how we should conduct ourselves in this seventh key area, we need to focus on several important words in this verse. David began by telling us what *not* to do. And he did it with emphasis. In the literal Hebrew (where they often moved words around in a sentence for impact), David wrote, "*A reprobate,* in his eyes, is despised."

Just who is a *reprobate?* It's someone who doesn't rate high in God's ranking system. It's a word that literally means "to cast off, to reject." In other words, it's something or someone of little value or weight.

Though it may sound harsh, it's a clear biblical fact that some people and their actions—especially toward Christ and the Holy Spirit—bring God's unquestioned rejection. Consider these chilling words of the prophet Jeremiah: "Cut off your hair and cast it away, and take up a lamentation on the bare heights; for the LORD has rejected and forsaken the generation of His wrath" (Jer. 7:29).

Like it or not, God is so committed to what is right that He rejects what is unmistakably wrong. So, when artists (funded by our tax dollars funneled through the National Endowment for the Arts) depict the Lord Jesus in gross acts of indecency in the name of "artistic expression," they're to be rejected. When pop singers or acid-tongued rock bands twist honorable names like Madonna or Jesus Christ, or promote names like the Living Dead or Cop Killers, they're biblical nobodies. When Emmy- or Academy Award–winning stars parade up to Capitol Hill in support of government-funded abortions or parade in downtown Hanoi at the same time our airmen are being tortured and killed just blocks away, they won't be called to get any awards God is ready to hand out.

There are people today—even well-known, highly publicized, wealthy, influential people—who are biblical reprobates. And David (and God) made it clear where they should stand in our value system.

Out of the Frying Pan . . .

Now, if you think that what we've said so far sounds awfully judgmental, it gets worse. Not only are certain people biblically certifiable reprobates, but David said we're to *despise* them.

Wait a minute before you throw down this book!

We told you in the beginning that David's words will lead us to solid ground, but that doesn't mean they aren't full of challenges. And this command is one of the most challenging of all. We know there are some men and women right now who are saying to themselves (or to the spouses they just woke up), "Wait a minute! Isn't this despising of a reprobate in direct violation of Christ's instructions to love and save the lost? How can you despise someone Christ died for?"

Good questions. And instead of writing off this part of Psalm 15 as just that "older testament" anomaly, we think David gave a good answer in carefully choosing the word he did—*despise*. That's because this word means to treat something "with little weight, *to undervalue it.*"

Did you catch that?

When we despise people (biblically), we don't cease to wish Christ's love would fill their hearts. We don't stop witnessing to them or calling them away from their sin and darkness and into God's light. But we also aren't required to subsidize their immoral behavior. (Remember the prodigal's father? He was always ready for his son to come home, but he didn't send him money while he was out of town to support his riotous living.) Nor should we elevate reprobates to a position of honor and respect in our eyes, *because someone else should already be sitting in that seat of honor.*

We can treat reprobates civilly and prayerfully without condoning their way of life and without putting their posters on our walls, wearing their T-shirts, or listening to their tapes because "their voices are *so good*" when their words are so wrong.

Let's face it. The world pushes pathology to the top all the time. Look at how low television networks are willing to go to get high ratings. Look at how sick our court system is as it caters to the rights of criminals and yet often ignores the rights of victims. Right now as you read this, a state court is deciding whether mass murderer Charles Manson's paintings can be sold to avid fans. It will also soon decide whether other convicted death-row inmates (like one who tried to kill a president) can sell their poetry and music on the open market. The sad thing is, in a world turned upside down, where we're taught to value the valueless, if these people's "works of art" are allowed outside prison walls, people will snap them up in a moment.

The world actively tries to squeeze more and more flawed, selfish, anti-Christian heroes onto its medal podium. But they've already missed the ceremony. They're hearing the anthem all right, but they don't know that the real medals have already been awarded. They've gone, and go today, to the second group of people pictured in Psalm 15:4.

Good Guys Should Finish First

Once again, in the original language, David switched the words around for emphasis. In this case, the second part of verse 4 should read, "*The ones who fear the Lord,* those should be honored."

Those who fear the Lord are His candidates for honor. *Fear* here means to have great respect for and utter awe and holy terror of the almighty God of the universe, who could single us out for annihilation but instead singles us out to receive the love of His Son. And *honor* is in direct contrast to the word *despise.*

When we're to honor someone who fears God, the word itself means "to be heavy" or "weighty." It's the idea of someone's being of great worth—a "heavyweight," who deserves high honor as a result. In other words, this seventh step in seeking solid ground is to have the right heroes *and to actively honor them*—to put weight and value on the right people, those who say the right things and do the right actions—because God is a righteous God.

> **Those who walk in righteousness ought to be honored. They ought to be looked up to. We should see *their* pictures on T-shirts!**

Those who walk in righteousness ought to be honored. They ought to be looked up to. We should see *their* pictures on T-shirts! Similarly, Jesus told us in Matthew 6:21, "For where your treasure is, there will your heart be also." When we treasure, or value, a person, that individual becomes an important influence in our lives.

This is a key principle for adults, but it has particular significance for the value-development process in children. Morris Massey, in his book *The People Puzzle,* argues that heroes we have when we're 10 years old are vital clues to who we'll become. It's at this age, he concludes from his studies, that children begin to look around for others whose lives are attractive to them, and those people become their role models.[1]

Stop and think for a few moments. Who were your heroes when you were 10 years old? Were they older brothers or sisters, a parent, a schoolteacher, a heroic soldier, a movie star, a professional athlete? Did those people affect the direction of your life in any way? We may not accomplish exactly what our heroes were doing when we were 10, but those individuals often greatly influence the direction of our lives.

That fact was forcefully driven home to me (Rick) one day when I was teaching a master's-level program to overseas missionaries. As a professor in a Christian university's extension program, I was in Taiwan, presenting the concept of values development. And on that day, I asked my adult missionary students the same question I've asked hundreds of students and guests at Forest Home stateside: "Who were your heroes when you were 10 years old?"

Out of the 15 students in my class, none had any trouble naming a significant someone. *And 11 of them were doing the same type of work as their heroes had been doing!* Some were pilots, some were teachers, and some were missionaries. But close to 75 percent had been heavily influenced at an early age by godly individuals who served as their role models.

Can you see how crucial it is that we expose our children to positive role models? We live in an era of countercultural heroes, from rap singers to arrogant athletes. But there are still hundreds of unsung heroes out there that we can hold up before our kids—an outstanding youth leader, a Christian teacher or coach, or the first people they model themselves after . . . us. We need to know who their heroes are and expose them to good and godly models.

God Treasures a Heart That Is Fully His, and So Should We

People who deserve to be honored often aren't world famous. But they're the right kind of heroes—the kind who get the gold medals in God's kingdom and should garner our honor and respect here on earth.

One such person is Chris Larkin. Chris is the mother-in-law of my (Rick's) best friend from high school. This woman was always there when I needed someone as a new Christian. She prayed with me when I was down, and she prayed for me that I'd find a godly mate and a place of ministry when school was out. People who lived in Lakewood, California, may not have known they were living next to a celebrity, but God and I did.

Such a couple are John's friends Lou and Celia Lutz. They're from Wichita, Kansas, but if you're also from Wichita, chances are you won't see them on the nightly news or the society page of Saturday's paper. That's because they're way too busy serving others for God.

Lou is a Dolly Madison bakery-goods deliveryman in the city, and Celia serves people as a dental hygienist . . . but that's just for starters. Lou and Celia are also active in their church; work hard at being loving parents to two wonderful kids, Sarah and Andy; drive to every soccer tournament they possibly can; run a woodcutting business; and were personally responsible for bringing in several nationally known Christian speakers and filling their city-wide seminars.

I (John) happened to be one of those speakers. It was one of the first engagements I'd done after I started my seminar called "The Blessing: Building Loving, Lasting Relationships." Without my saying a thing, Lou and Celia saw that I couldn't possibly put on the seminar by myself. Yet, being in a new ministry, I didn't have the funds to hire someone to help set up, run, and take down the seminar.

That's when they prayed hard, talked to their children and Lou's nonchurch-attending boss, and got nothing but green lights to give me a call and make me an incredible offer. Instead of my lugging books for a book table to a seminar in Dallas, Lou gets in early the first day and does it. That leaves me time to spend the afternoon praying and getting ready to speak. And instead of my showing up extra early to arrange the registration tables and train volunteers for a seminar in Fresno, Celia does that. I can concentrate on teaching God's Word instead of collecting tickets.

Lou and Celia do all this behind the scenes, and they do it free of charge. All it costs Encouraging Words is their airfare, room, and food, and what they give back is worth millions to me. When it comes to honoring those who fear the Lord, Lou and Celia are in my hall of fame.

Is all this talk about everyday heroes bringing someone to mind? Good! For if you'll recall, we mentioned earlier that *honor* is an active word. It begs to be applied. It seeks a worthy place to rest—like on that teacher who never heard that she made the biggest impression of anyone on your life . . . that parent who doesn't ask for your thanks but deserves it daily . . . that boss who was a life-changing mentor . . . or that employee or friend who's been faithful since way past forever.

Write in the space below the name (or names) of someone who helped you significantly in your Christian or personal life.

Your Unsung Hero's Name

If you penciled in a name, congratulations! You've just entered that person in the Official Unsung Heroes Hall of Fame. Why don't you pick up the phone or a pen and call or write your hero with a word of thanks. If the person has passed away, take some time to thank God for his or her memory and loving help.

We'd love for you to do something else as well. Write down why this person is so worthy of honor for fearing the Lord, and send us a note about it. We'll compile all the "God's Unsung Heroes" stories that are sent to us, and who knows . . . that may be the title of a future heart-warming book!

You say you're clear on what the passage says, but you still need some specifics on how to put honoring actions into practice? Let's look at several ways you can make this part of Psalm 15 your personal property.

Putting Honor into Action

Below is a list of practical ways you can put honor into action. It is by no means exhaustive, but it will give you a good start in developing this part of a rock-solid lifestyle.

1. Outstanding books: Read books that tell true stories of how God has used and/or helped individuals in various aspects of life.

2. Edifying videos: Watch some of the growing number of great videos available, ranging from sermons to testimonies to kids' adventure stories (e.g., the McGee & Me series).

3. Successful Christians: Develop a relationship with those who have succeeded in life and who attribute their success to their Christian lifestyle. Use them as role models for yourself and your children.

4. Overcomers: Likewise, talk to and learn from those who have overcome some difficult situation.

5. Missionaries: When missionaries are home on furlough, invite them for a meal. Help your family discover what heroes missionaries are. Develop a personal relationship between your family and a missionary family through writing letters, visits, and so on.

6. Speakers: Make it a point to hear a variety of speakers at camps, seminars, and conferences. If an opportunity arises for personal contact with a speaker (meals, conversations, etc.), take advantage of it.

7. Provide experiences for your family that will help them appreciate what's important in God's economy:

    a. Short-term missions: Go as a family or send your older children on a short-term missions project.
    b. Evangelistic outreach: Participate in an outreach project sponsored by your church or another Christian organization.
    c. Community project: Get involved in a local community project that carries out a Christian principle (e.g., caring for the needy).
    d. Church involvement: Be active in your local church, using the spiritual gifts God has given the members of your family.

May We Never Forget Betsie

As we close this chapter, let's take a look at one more example of a life well spent. Betsie was a brave and kind woman living with her family when the fighting began in her country during the Second World War. Then came something worse . . . the rounding up and even the execution of many Jews in her city.

Betsie couldn't just sit by.

She was a strong Christian with a passion for the Lord and a willingness to stand up and do something she felt was right, even if it was fraught with danger. In the face of Nazi threats of terrible reprisals, she hid Jews in her home who were trying not to end up in Hitler's infamous extermination camps.

But one horrible day in 1944, Betsie got to see the inside of one of those camps herself. She was arrested after having been sold out by a Nazi sympathizer, and she found herself on her way to one of the worst camps, a place called Ravensbrück.

She had to endure the terror of being captured at gunpoint, then see that increase a hundredfold when she was sent to the concentration camp. The huge room there contained harsh overhead lights, a pathetic pile of clothes and shoes taken from women and children who were long since gone . . . and the walking dead. There was also the shame of walking naked past cruel guards. Later, she was beaten, starved, and left untreated when fever and dysentery hit.

But Betsie didn't stop loving God. In fact, she loved Him more. And it was in large part her love for the Savior that inspired someone there with her to hang on and stay strong.

The world took little notice the day Betsie died. But her sister, Corrie Ten Boom, did. And while Corrie's story of faith, love, and forgiveness (mentioned briefly at the end of chapter 13) warmed the hearts of thousands across the world, few remember or give thanks for another hero—someone deserving high honor and great respect—a Christian martyr named Betsie.

Next we'll look at the second half of verse 4 and see how solid ground also comes from a specific, scriptural way of making important agreements.

Reflections
Well-Placed Respect

1. What image does the word *honor* convey to you? In your own words, how do you define it?

2. What influences in your life (friends, entertainers, athletes, teachers, etc.) can cause you to follow after or honor the wrong things? What do you plan to do about it?

3. John and Rick asked you to consider who your heroes were when you were 10 years old. Who were they? Why did you look up to them? In what ways have you followed their examples?

4. Who are your heroes today? How have your criteria for choosing heroes changed since you were 10?

Chapter 15

THE EIGHTH KEY

Choosing Commitment Over Convenience

He swears to his own hurt, and does not change. . . .

The sprawling international headquarters of Encouraging Words ministry (all 814 square feet of it) is located in a business district called the Scottsdale Air Park in Arizona. That's because the building that houses my (John's) ministry, and many buildings like it, is parked next to a major commuter airport. All the planes landing and taking off make a wonderful distraction from actually having to work. And during breakfast or lunch, you can get an even closer look at a wonderful airport restaurant called The Left Seat.

It was there, at that restaurant, that I saw the jet. Like dozens of others harbored at Scottsdale Airport, it was a Lear. And it was on display—no doubt about it. Many people in the restaurant that day were talking about the new owner who was just getting ready to take it up for a spin.

What many people didn't know was the "spin" the owner had put on hundreds of others to purchase it.

You see, that plane came at a much higher price than just the $2 million paid to Lear. It had taken untold millions out of the pockets of many good, salt-of-the-earth, hardworking people who had unknowingly financed it. As I sat and enjoyed breakfast with my children, I realized that it had likely taken real meals out of some real children's mouths.

Let me back up a second to put this incident in context. The year was 1986. The real estate market in Arizona had basked in the inflationary economy of the 1970s and grown out of control in the first half of the 1980s. Finally, the inevitable adjustments of an overpriced market had no choice but to make their move. In 1986, unsecured loans by savings and loans and undercollateralized notes from banks caused the market to crash like a house of cards. New-home contracts were at a standstill, and you couldn't give away the surplus office space.

When the real estate market started to collapse, there were only a handful of gigantic developers but hundreds of small fish. The little guys fell through the cracks in the first wave of the adjustment. The big guys struggled to hang on. Before it was over, however, even they had to succumb to the inevitable.

Most of them finished the houses they had begun, sold them at a loss, and then slid into obscurity to lick their wounds. Some couldn't even do that. One of them, *one of the biggest,* decided to call his tax attorneys and see what he could salvage.

When I say this builder was big, I mean he was BIG. At one time he had hundreds of subcontractors working for him. Most of them were men and women with little companies, and they actually built his homes.

Those subcontractors had stacks of invoices in to this man for the materials they'd already paid for themselves and installed in his houses. They had payrolls to meet, reputations to maintain, and families to feed. It was imperative that they get paid in full and soon.

But then the tax attorneys met. They outlined the options for this huge home builder. They explained the nuances of the bankruptcy codes. They spelled out the ramifications for all the people who waited in the wings with their invoices. And within days, he was in front of a bankruptcy judge filing a petition for protection from his creditors and subcontractors. It was granted with the condition that he would expedite a solution in a timely manner.

It didn't take him long to make his announcement. The banks would get back the land and all the unfinished projects, and the subcontractors would be paid 40 cents on the dollar.

When I read the article about it in the paper, I remember shaking my head in sadness for all those good, hardworking people. One small contractor whom I knew and who went to our church had opened his paper to see that this man's actions had just put him out of business. At 40 cents on the dollar, there was no way he or dozens like him could survive. They couldn't pay their materials invoices, let alone their outstanding payrolls. It was just a matter of days before their creditors would start repossessing their trucks, equipment, tools, and, in some cases, their homes.

I realize there are times when bankruptcy is the only option. Our laws governing it have their roots in the Old Testament. It was a form of grace granted to people who fell on hard times and had no way of digging out without help. But they were never designed as a way to hide one man's fortune and rob others of the basics.

What does this have to do with the Lear jet that taxied down the airport runway? The day after the announcement that he would not pay his subcontractors all he owed them, Mr. Humongus Home Builder had bought his little jet *for cash*. That money could and should have gone to those to whom he had promised it.

The Hard Cost of Keeping Our Promises

Psalm 15 outlines 10 characteristics of people who will never be shaken. Interestingly, when David listed these 10 traits, they all fell into tidy groupings—except this one. There are the first three positives we've already looked at. Then come the three negatives we've just examined. The seventh key contains its own contrast as we've just seen. And now, like an island of emphasis, David slipped in this eighth requirement for rock-solid living. It calls us to follow through on commitments we make . . . period—even if it hurts. Put in the words of Psalm 15, "He swears to his own hurt, and does not change."

You can pick up different translations, and they use slightly different sets of words, but they all have the same bottom line: People who stand on God's solid ground swear even to their own hurt. They may not be perfect, but they do all they can to keep from breaking commitments and hurting others.

That jet parked on the tarmac was just one man's way of thumbing his nose at responsibility and the words of Psalm 15. But he wasn't the first.

A Cord of Seven Strands

Back in biblical times, there was a problem with what some people were doing at the time of sacrifice. Certain men and women were making a public pledge of, say, a spotless lamb. But when the time came to actually offer up the sacrifice, they swapped a skinny, 10-year-old, blind billy goat for that promised beautiful, young lamb.

In the Book of Leviticus, we read, "Now if it is an animal of the kind which men can present as an offering to the LORD . . . he shall not replace it or exchange it, a good for a bad, or a bad for a good" (Lev. 27:9–10). In other words, if you made a pledge before the Lord, you were to hold to it and not swap a clear loser for a winner you'd committed.

That high standard is clearly seen in two words in the command of Psalm 15:4: "He *swears* to his own hurt, and does not *change*." What does that mean for all of us who live in a culture of compromise and broken promises? First, consider the Hebrew word translated "to swear." One of the wonderful things about the Hebrew language is how it often uses pictures behind many of its words. For example, the major word in Hebrew for anger is "nostrils," for the flaring of an angry person's nostrils (or even how they turn red) when he's mad. For fear, the word is "kidneys" . . . for obvious reasons.

The picture behind this word translated "to swear" is classic. Literally, what David said here is, "He *seven's himself*, and will not change."

Seven's himself?

Try an experiment. Go out to the garage and get some kite string left over from last spring's outing with the kids (or grandkids). Now pull out about a three-foot length and wrap the ends around each hand several times. Then, using all your strength, see if you can quickly pull on the string and break it. Although it might dig into your palms a little, most people can accomplish this task.

But now try something that will likely defeat even the most muscular. Take *seven* three-foot lengths of kite string and twist them together. Then try to break the cord you've made.

Can you see now (whether you actually went to the garage or not) what it means, biblically, to swear to something? It means that you're saying, "I'm wrapping up this agreement in earnest. It's something that can stand the press and pull of whatever comes, because it's a sevenfold strand." Sevening ourselves pictures something strong, lasting, and unbreakable.

Then toss in the second important word in the verse, "He swears to his own hurt, and does not *change*," and watch the standard for our commitments go even higher.

When the Price Is the Price

The word *change* also has a powerful picture behind it. It literally means "to hunt, or barter for food." In a primarily barter economy like that of the Old Testament, the art of bartering was honed to a fine edge. I (John) discovered just how ingrained bargaining is in that part of the world one night in the Old City of Jerusalem.

I had the privilege of leading a tour of Israel several years ago. One night, I happened to be out walking with my good friend Mike Burnidge. Our tour guide had taken us to various sites that day, and most of our party were exhausted and opted to hit the sack. That left Mike and me to try to track down a few last-minute souvenirs before the shops closed.

In the Old City of Jerusalem, the streets are narrow and lined with hundreds of tiny shops. It was getting quite late, and Mike was still in one shop when I walked next door just as the lights were being turned off. "Oh, I'm sorry," I said to the proprietor. "I didn't know you were closed."

"Oh, no!" he assured me. "I was just checking the lights. We're not closed."

As I came inside, the shopkeeper asked if I was looking for anything in particular. That's when my eye fell on one of the most beautiful carved wooden figurines of Moses I'd ever seen. The only problem was, it stood over three feet high, was solid olive wood, and had a price tag on it that could have funded a third of my trip.

"Yeah," I said. "I want to buy this statue here. *It's not exactly what I'm looking for.* But it'll do."

Obviously, I'd already been in a few shops, where I'd cut my teeth on the haggling that's expected in that country. But in my mind, I really wasn't bargaining. He would have had to cut his price in half, and then in half again, before I'd remotely think about purchasing it. And even then, how could I fit it into an already overstuffed backpack and lug it around Israel and on to Rome?

But I learned something that night. First, you do your best bargaining when you have absolutely nothing to lose if you don't get the item. And second, there's a cultural tradition for shop owners in Jerusalem that it's bad luck not to sell the last customer something.

With both those things (unknowingly) going for me, I proceeded to kill some time until Mike caught up with me by seeing just how low this shopkeeper would go on this masterpiece. "I wouldn't pay *that* price for it," I said. "I wouldn't give you one-*tenth* of what you're charging."

And from there, you can imagine what the next half hour held. Offer and counteroffer. Bargaining that would have made the top peddler in any Arabian bazaar proud if I had been his student. In fact, without question, it was the best bit of haggling I had ever done in my life . . . *only I didn't know I was bargaining!* I was just having fun until my friend came back.

When Mike did arrive, I walked out of the shop with him in mock disgust, and the shop owner pursued me down the street, literally with tears in his eyes! He asked me to come back and make him one final offer, so I did, knowing full well he would reject it.

But he accepted it!

"One more thing," I said.

"What?" he said, throwing up his hands.

"You know that staff Moses is holding in his hands?" (It was a long, wooden staff with a serpent's head carved on it.) "I want you to throw in an extra staff just in case this one breaks."

He did throw it in . . . and the original staff *did* break while being carted across the ocean. But I had bargained my way down to a figure that even our tour guide said was pretty good. "In fact, that's *really good* for an American." he said. "It takes a long time for them to mass-produce those."

Even today, if you have the chance to visit the world headquarters of Encouraging Words, you'll be permitted to see Moses standing right next to my desk, with an unbroken staff. And I still think it's the best-looking mass-produced copy of a reproduction ever made.

That's literally what the word *change* meant in biblical times: The final agreement was "up for grabs." There was a price, but it was negotiable. There may have been words spoken, hands shaken, or even agreements penned on paper, but everyone knew there was a "changeable" bottom line.

For David, however, the bottom line was the bottom line. Like a strand of seven cords, it was to be unbreakable. And instead of being bargained for, it was to be held at face value.

Can you see now how the man who purchased the Lear jet stepped off solid ground when he stepped into that bankruptcy agreement? His commitments were as flimsy as one strand of kite string, and *everything*— including his credibility—was negotiable.

There's got to be a better way to treat people and commitments. And there is, as David so clearly asserted. Realize, however, that like the tough standards of righteousness, integrity, and truth, as well as the uncompromising call to avoid slander, evil, and reproach, keeping our promises will often cost us something. But it may also hold unseen rewards.

Pass the Coffee, Please

I (Rick) remember a particularly demanding day at the end of which I came home to Kathy exhausted. It had been a morning of meetings, an afternoon of crises, an evening of appointments, and a night of last-minute details. I finally found my way home late that night. When I slipped into bed, I was beyond tired. I could have qualified as the poster child for the absolutely exhausted.

It was already past midnight. Kathy had retired to bed hours earlier. As I slipped in next to her, I thought that the last thing I'd remember would be closing my eyes before the alarm went off the next morning. But wouldn't you know it . . . with my head just two-thirds of the way down on my pillow, I remembered something else I needed to do. An alarm was sounding somewhere in the back corridors of my mind. *Don't you have a speaking engagement tomorrow morning?* it said in that persistent, sleep-robbing voice.

No . . . it couldn't be.

I did remember that conversation I'd had with Kathy's boss. But that had been months ago! He had asked me to speak at the Christian business-men's breakfast he hosted and to give an evangelistic message. I recalled saying I'd be glad to do it but that he must write me with the details if he really wanted me to do it. We had talked vaguely about the date and time, but he'd never sent a confirmation letter. Yet, as I got up from bed and stumbled into the kitchen to look at my Day-Timer, sure enough, there it was. Tomorrow was the morning for the meeting . . . or was it?

Maybe they weren't meeting. Maybe he had talked to someone else. Maybe I needed to be there just in case.

At an hour when I would have much rather been in a warm bed instead of sitting at the kitchen table pounding down stale coffee, I began to put together a message for the next morning. Why? Because Psalm 15 kept ringing in my head: "He swears to his own hurt, and does not change."

I prepared my message. Finally, I was able to get to sleep, only to arise four hours later at 5:30 A.M. so I could make the long drive to the restaurant—a place I was sure would be inhabited by only a few off-shift police-men and chronic early risers. But I was wrong. The back room was *filled* when I arrived. Much to my surprise, they had a banner that read,

"Welcome, Mr. Hicks!" and a seat waiting for me at the head table.

That morning, I told a large group the story of how I became a Christian (which I also told you earlier in this book). And at the end of the message, as people began to file out, a father and son came over to me. They explained that they had been invited by their boss to the breakfast and hadn't been sure of what to expect. But after I started giving my message, they found out why they were supposed to be there. You see, God had brought them there to introduce them to Himself. They told me that when I had offered each man the chance to receive Jesus Christ into his heart, they had both prayed along with me. What a wonderful moment for all of us!

Many times since that meeting, I've wondered what would have happened if a few words inscribed by a ruddy, harp-playing, often hot-tempered shepherd hadn't kept me awake half the night.

Sometimes we don't have any control over what people are determined to say about us. But we do control what we feel when we look at ourselves in the mirror.

"He swears to his own hurt, and does not change."

It may keep you awake. It's costly in terms of time, effort, and perhaps even money to keep your promises . . . but it's also one of the greatest assets you can have in your life. When you do get to sleep, it lets you sleep better. When it's practiced in a marriage, it warms your spouse's heart. When it's followed through in commitments kept with your children, it gets them behind you more enthusiastically. When it's time to stand up and be counted at work, it causes your voice to have a greater impact.

Character is far more important than reputation. Sometimes we don't have any control over what people are determined to say about us. But we do control what we feel when we look at ourselves in the mirror. That's why we can't afford to cash in when it comes to our character. People who break promises have to spend a lot of time avoiding people, cataloging deceptions, and attacking the folks who get close enough to ask the hard questions. People who lack character lose more than they gain taking the easy way out when they renege on a promise. It's just a matter of time until a life of broken commitments meets its Waterloo. Just ask Judas.

You see, like the other nine keys presented in Psalm 15, this one offers us such solid footing because it puts us on holy ground. God takes promises seriously, even if many around us don't.

God is the One "with whom there is no variation" (James 1:17).

He says of Himself, "For I, the LORD, do not change" (Mal. 3:6).

He says to us, "For He Himself has said, 'I will never desert you, nor will I ever forsake you'" (Heb. 13:5).

If we're to be like Christ, we must be promise keepers. And we know that's incredibly difficult, especially in a world where we may be linked with a person in business (or, unfortunately, even marriage) who tramples on the commitments we hold sacred.

When Other People Trample Our Commitments

I (John) have a wonderful mother who I think would win any award as the best single parent ever. (Of course, I am slightly prejudiced.) When she was only 20, she married a handsome young man who wooed her, won over her family, whisked her away after their wonderful wedding, and then left her for another woman in less than a year.

Then came my father. It was a few years later, and he was a returning war hero, complete with the Bronze Star won at Guadalcanal and a bronzed tan from playing golf with his clients in sunny Arizona. He, too, courted, wooed, and committed himself for a lifetime to my mother. Yet, when I was only two months old, he also departed for "greener pastures," leaving my mother to raise three young sons on her own.

We know there are times when the reality of a fallen world rips a wedding certificate or signed contract in half, but that doesn't mean we have to be the one to rip it up. Ecclesiastes 5:4–5 says, "When you make a vow to God, do not be late in paying it, for He takes no delight in fools. Pay what you vow! It is better that you should not vow than that you should vow and not pay." Those are strong words strongly stated. But even in the face of bad situations, we're to hold the line on doing what's right.

What Steps Does a Promise Keeper Take?

Today, a promise keeper might look like any one of the 62,000 men in Indianapolis or the 68,000 men in the Thunder Dome in Tampa. Thousands of men across our country are gathering together to make a promise to God and to their families that they'll be the men God wants them to be. Women shouldn't be jealous or resentful of men attending these rallies either. After all, women have been faithfully keeping one-sided promises far too long—we men are just playing catch-up in most cases.

Whether we're male or female, we need to follow David's words in Psalm 15. So, let us give you three suggestions for making promise keeping an everyday part of your home life.

1. Fulfill your promises in a timely manner.

Before you make a promise, have every intention of fulfilling your words. Making a promise casually is an invitation to break it.

I (John) knew a father who promised his son he'd build him a fort in their backyard. The son kept asking about the fort, and the father kept promising that some day . . . soon . . . they'd get it made. Finally, the father did get around to building it. In fact, he spent two entire weekends working long into the night. But by then, his boy had turned 13, and he never stuck his head inside it.

Nobody likes to be called a fool. But that's exactly what God's Word says about someone who doesn't follow through (see Eccles. 5:4). Wise people will make sure their words reflect reality.

2. Add up the realistic cost before you go to war.

In Luke 14:31, we're told it's a wise king who counts the cost before he goes to war. What that means is that you should calculate first, then commit. And while you're adding, you'd better add up the downside risk and the worst-case scenario and not make a commitment unless you're ready to pay that price.

3. Be accountable.

One of the best ways to make sure you're keeping your promises is to give a couple of trusted friends the right to get in your face and call you on the carpet when you start to vacillate over the promises you've made. In the long run, character can't survive without loving accountability.

A Shining Example of a Promise Kept

Remember the man who flew off in his jet? The only time people looked up to him was at takeoff. But there's someone else I (John) know whom I can't help but admire. His name is Dave Cavan, and he's a promise keeper—one of those men who, like David, sought to swear to his own hurt and not change.

Dave was also one of those big guys on the real estate playing field back in 1986. In fact, in his investment portfolio, he had commercial property worth over $200 *million*. He owed the banks half of that amount. The rest was considered his bottom line. There are not many guys in that league.

But as I mentioned earlier, 1986 was the year the real estate market in the southwestern United States started to turn upside down. Interest rate pressures created massive problems, which caused panic. Within months, Dave realized something awful was happening to his properties. He rolled up his sleeves and dove into the middle of the crisis. He came in earlier and worked later. He pushed pencils and brooms himself. He crunched numbers and carried out the trash. But nothing could stop what was happening.

Within a year, he found himself facing the exact same nightmare every other builder and developer was facing—including the man with the Lear jet. But there was one big difference between Dave and "Sky King." Dave believed that handshakes mean something—that his word was a witness to his two sons coming up in the business and to his Lord.

In an unprecedented move, Dave got all his bankers in the same room and made a promise to pay back *all* he owed them. They proceeded to tell him that he was categorically nuts and rejected his offer.

He persisted.

So did they.

But eventually, he worked out an arrangement with each one to make good on his commitments.

Meanwhile, there were a lot of good people who had done work for Dave and who needed to be paid. Dave and his godly wife, Karen (who helps me with the many counseling letters we receive here at Encouraging Words), sat in their sprawling home on the golf course. They owned it free and clear. It was filled with gorgeous furniture, precious heirlooms, and exotic toys of the rich and famous. They looked at the amount of money they owed all the people who had put their confidence in them. They discussed the advice their attorney had given them about bankruptcy. They, too, knew they could use the tax code to protect their personal fortune.

But they couldn't escape that number at the bottom of the page and all the families it represented. With a resolve that only hearts filled with integrity can muster, they took each other's hand, looked in each other's eyes, and nodded to each other in approval of one way they could cut down the debt.

It would all have to go. Every bit of it.

They would sell the house and every stick of furniture. As far as they were concerned, none of it was theirs anymore. It belonged to the families to whom they still owed money. And so, a short time later, they held the biggest garage sale Scottsdale had ever seen. Hundreds of people crowded their cars into the side streets of the posh neighborhood. There in the midst of it all were Dave and Karen—marking prices; watching family heirlooms being carted away; saving the pictures of the kids but wondering if there would be anything to leave them. Yet, they were two people who didn't just talk about integrity. They had wrapped seven cords around their commitment to Christ and others and sworn to their own hurt.

It took that garage sale and a few more years of hard work, but today, Dave has paid back every borrowed dollar to every person and financial institution. And by the way, he still builds the best houses and developments you can find. Once again he could pay cash for a Lear jet and fly it with a clean conscience. But image isn't what matters to him.

Is it painful to keep our promises? *You bet!*

Embarrassing sometimes? *Absolutely!*

Worth it all? *Without a doubt!*

Any regrets? *None!*

That's the bottom line of being men and women of our word. It isn't easy. We pay a hefty price. But when we get to the other side of the right choice, we're standing on rock-solid, heaven-trod soil. It's the same ground that supports a ninth key . . . an admonition for even us penny-pinchers to not go into the loan shark business.

Reflections

Choosing Commitment Over Convenience

1. Think of a time when a parent or someone else made and kept a promise to you. How did that make you feel?

2. Recall a time you made a promise that you later wished you could break. Did you keep it or break it? Why?

3. What reasons, if any, would justify the breaking of a promise? Explain your answer.

4. If the need arose to break a promise you had made, how would you communicate that fact to the other person?

Chapter 16

THE NINTH KEY

Financial Fairness

He does not put out his money at interest. . . .

astor, they're coming to repossess our home." The voice on the other end of the line was filled with emotion. "I can't believe it."

As I (John) listened to the story, I couldn't believe it either. After all, Janet and her husband, Bobby, had to be the best-dressed couple in the young marrieds' class my wife and I led. Both had next-to-new cars, and they lived in a charming new home. In fact, their house was so big and pretty, Cindy and I hoped our starter home would grow up to look like it someday.

Sure, I'll have to admit I was a little envious that Bobby had *two* of his own metal bats that he brought to the softball games. And they did have those NBA season tickets, but they were upper-deck seats, and it *was* an expansion team.

Plus, they'd only been married three years. Kids hadn't come along yet, and the two of them looked to have endless potential. How could they have gone from being the "toast of the town" to standing in the bread line in three years?

The answer was interesting. Try 21 percent interest.

Bobby and Janet had both come from upscale homes with doting parents. They met at a private college and had a wedding ceremony fit for the monarch of a small country. Armed with great expectations of future earnings, they set out in three years to accumulate what had taken their parents 30 years to collect. But in their rush to reach the top, the ground they stood on went from marble floors to a Florida sinkhole.

As it turns out, Bobby and Janet had borrowed money from both sets of parents to get into their new house, and they even charged part of the closing fees on a credit card. They'd furnished everything from curtains to china to chairs on the installment plan. They had purchased their cars on no-money-down "deferred" payment plans. And they'd even set up revolving credit lines at no less than six of the best department stores.

Then along came 1980. On September 14, 1980, interest rates soared, with the *prime rate* getting up to 21.5 percent. Their variable-rate no-ceiling home mortgage that had been such a bargain in 1977 suddenly gave them a lot more than they bargained for—namely, a house payment (on top of all their other escalating payments) that had gone up and up and up . . . rising along with their creditors' anger, which was now expressed in threatening calls and letters of eviction.

Amazingly, in just 36 months, they'd accumulated more than $27,000 in consumer and credit card debt. And that was besides what they owed on their house.

You could say that at least they looked good in getting into so much debt. But in reality, their actions left them with an ugly, damaged witness in the community and nearly destroyed their marriage.

That must be why King David gave us this ninth aspect of standing on solid ground: "He does not put out his money at interest. . . ." Not quite. For although Scripture is replete with calls to wise financial accountability, David wasn't talking here about the inherent dangers of a person or couple *borrowing* money, but of *lending* it.

Now, before you think this chapter isn't for you, take a closer look. It doesn't apply only if you have enough money to lend out, nor was it written only for your mortgage banker friend. What David meant by not lending money at interest in his day is fully applicable in each of our lives today.

Is David Calling for the Collapse of the Current Banking System or Something Else?

Remember: Psalm 15 is giving us clear directions on how to put our feet on solid ground. And linked right with the other instructions is the admonition not to loan our money at interest. So, what does that mean? Is David calling for the collapse of the current banking system? Do "real" Christian men and women sin when they take out a loan? If so, do they also sin when they deposit their money in a bank, which in turn loans their money at interest to others?

For centuries, such questions have been debated by the best church leaders and scholars. The issue even made it into one of Shakespeare's plays. In *The Merchant of Venice* (act 1, scene 3), his character Shylock described someone he despised . . . a Christian.

> How like a fawning publican he looks!
> I hate him for he is a Christian:
> But more for that in low simplicity
> He lends out money *gratis*, and brings down
> The rate of usance here with us in Venice.

Imagine a Christian lender today charging no interest on home or business loans—and imagine lines stretching as far as the eye can see! What did David mean here? And why is it so vital that we still heed his admonition if we're to set our feet on solid ground?

We don't claim to be able to settle a centuries-old conflict in the Christian community in a few pages, but we do think Scripture is clear on several things. First, we can tell you the interesting background of what the word for *interest* actually means. Second, we'll tell you what we know is the only type of loan that would get past a Hebrew loan officer in David's day. And third, we'll see how, in fully understanding this verse, David's injunction has as much to say about putting on a heart of compassion as it does about our cash flow or credit balance. So, let's begin by looking at the word *interest* itself as we seek to understand what David called us to in this verse.

When Taking a Bite Is a Crime

One of the most appealing characters in public service ads is McGruff the Crime Dog, who urges television viewers to "take a bite out of crime." And in the ancient world David lived in, interest rates themselves were a crime.

Take the Babylonians, for example. The rate they charged for loans of grain was a measly 33.5 percent. The Assyrians, another neighboring nation, set interest rates at *141 percent* in their day. The famed Code of Hammurabi sought to place limitations on interest rates in the ancient world, bringing them down to the double digits at least for the poor.[1]

Perhaps it was rates like those that led an ancient rabbi to write in the Talmud, "It is better to sell your daughter into slavery than to borrow money on interest!"[2] Without question, price gouging is reflected in the meaning of the two primary words for *interest* recorded in the Bible.

The first Hebrew term is the word *nesek,* and it's found here in Psalm 15. It literally means "to take a bite out of something; to bite off." Many people, like Bobby and Janet above, who had amassed a huge credit card debt, have learned the hard way how out-of-control interest can take a literal bite out of their livelihood.

The second Hebrew word, *tarbit,* means "to increase, to grow," which is used elsewhere in Scripture. But both terms seem to be used interchangeably. Again, looking to one of Israel's neighbors, we see a related Accadian word, *hubullu,* which means "to injure, ill-treat, oppress, be in debt." There's no doubt that the high interest of David's time caused people to have a "hulla-baloo" (an American word for what happens when we actually read the annual interest rates on the back of our credit card statements).

Just from the definitions of those words, you can begin to see the meaning of *interest* in Psalm 15:5. In the Trent-Hicks translation, we'd render it "a rate charged to someone that continues to grow until it takes a bite out of the person."

So, is David saying that a person is to make no loans at all? Or that it's permissible to make loans but not charge interest? Or is he saying something else? In a way, the answer to all three questions is yes. Here's what we mean.

Getting Past the "Loan Officer" in Ancient Israel

Regardless of what other nations were doing around Israel, God's people were always called to a higher standard. God didn't want dishonoring price gouging going on, especially with a certain group of people. Look closely at the words Moses recorded in the Book of Exodus: "If you lend money to My people, to the poor among you, you are not to act as a creditor to him; you shall not charge him interest" (Exod. 22:25).

See any particular qualification to who receives a loan? If you missed it, just turn to the Book of Leviticus: "Now in case a countryman of yours becomes poor and his means with regard to you falter, then you are to sustain him, like a stranger or a sojourner, that he may live with you. Do not take usurious interest from him, but revere your God, that your countryman may live with you" (Lev. 25:35–36).

If you're beginning to see a pattern—good! For that qualification of being *poor* before you could obtain a loan in Scripture is further defined in another passage in Deuteronomy: "You shall not charge interest to your countrymen. . . . You may charge interest to a foreigner, but to your countryman, you shall not charge interest" (Deut. 23:19–20).

The person, then, who could get past a Hebrew loan officer in David's day was a member of God's people and a man or woman who had become so poor that he or she literally needed assistance with the basics of life.

Scripture doesn't forbid all uses of interest. Remember how our Lord Jesus rebuked someone for not gaining a return on his investment? In the parable of the talents, He rewarded those whose investments grew. But the man who had buried his talent He chastised with the words, "Then you ought to have put my money in the bank, and . . . I would have received my money back with interest" (Matt. 25:27).

Yet, investment interest is not what David had in mind in Psalm 15. The command not to charge interest referred to "taking a bite" out of the little a destitute person had to live on. Charging the poor interest wasn't an exercise in wise stewardship but in exploitation. But again, unless we just happen to own our own banks, how does David's command relate to us?

We can think of three things each of us needs to take away from this passage—three things that can help us increase our sensitivity while decreasing our chances of hurting a brother.

1. God has a clear place in His heart for the poor and needy.

Several years ago, Focus on the Family asked me (John) to describe a special Christmas memory as part of an audio collage of people's experiences that the ministry was putting together for the holidays. My mind instantly went back to when I was eight years old.

It was a Christmas when everything seemed to have gone wrong. My mother was in the hospital in Indiana due to complications with her arthritis. My twin brother was going through tests for a stomach problem, and my older brother had been sent with him to my aunt's house to keep him company. Since my father had left the family when I was two months old, that left my grandmother and me to hold down the fort that Christmas.

Despite all the family health problems, I remember the anticipation building as Christmas drew near. I had my list of toys and "guy stuff" that I'd long since turned in to my grandmother—along with innumerable added extras. And although I realized I wouldn't get *everything* on my list, there were a few things I just knew were sure to end up under the tree.

Christmas Eve came, and I remember sitting down with my grand-mother to a scrumptious meal: turkey, "smashed" potatoes, corn, dressing, gravy, and her incredible chocolate cake. It had struck me as odd, however, that nothing had been put out early under the tree. But so much that Christmas was different, I dismissed it as something Grandmother hadn't had time to do. Obviously, she'd been busy keeping tabs on the dispersed family and taking care of me. But I was sure Santa would be hard at work wrapping presents after I pretended to go to sleep.

Later that night, I walked down the hall and heard someone crying softly. When I peeked into my grandmother's room, she had tears in her eyes. And in a few moments, I did, too. It turned out that with all the medical bills and all the travel and related expenses, my Christmas present that year was the meal I'd eaten earlier that night.

I remember being deeply hurt at first. But then I saw how much more pain lined my grandmother's tear-stained face. That evening, we didn't talk about what we *didn't* have. We talked about what we *did* have—a close family that loved each other, the love of God to warm us on a cold (for Arizona) Christmas night, and the hope of a bright future with everyone back together and healthy in the new year.

I've never had another Christmas like that. It taught me many indelible lessons about what mattered most—about what the greatest gift is that we cele-brate and about how God can keep a family together even when circumstances push it far apart. I also gained a brief snapshot of what it means to be poor. We weren't poor in the way that many around the world, or even in our own coun-try, would count poverty. But for me that night, I felt as if God had filled up our small measure of poverty with an extra measure of His love. And there's a reason for that. Namely, God has a special place in His heart for the poor.

In the Old Testament, God went to great lengths to communicate His care and concern for the truly poor. For example, when harvest time came, one corner of each field was to be left unharvested for the destitute to come in and glean (see Lev. 19:9). Remember how this led to a budding romance between a poor woman of faith named Ruth and a field owner named Boaz?

What's more, every seven years, the farmers in the land were to leave their fields alone, neither planting nor harvesting, so that the land itself could have a season of "rest" like God's people. However, while a farmer would put up stores for that period, what of the poor? They didn't have storerooms from past harvests that they could turn to. But they did have a compassionate God who provided for them by commanding that whatever grew of its own accord in the farmer's fields was to be reaped by the poor alone that year (see Exod. 23:11).

God's special concern for the poor was why it wouldn't be right to strap them with double-digit-plus interest. And it wouldn't be right for another reason as well.

2. God's people had already spent years in slavery.

In the Book of Leviticus, we read, "And if a countryman of yours becomes so poor with regard to you that he sells himself to you, you shall not subject him to a slave's service. He shall be with you as a hired man" (Lev. 25:39–40). Why prohibit slavery? Because God's people had already spent their share of dreadful years in bondage. And in an act foreshadowing Christ's work on the Cross, He raised up a great deliverer named Moses, who brought His people out of slavery and into freedom.

God didn't want to see people whom He had delivered from bondage enter it again, and He knew that's exactly what poverty could do to a person. If someone owed another person a great debt, it might be tempting to have the debtor bound over to you as a slave. But God would have nothing to do with that.

In fact, showing incredible mercy, God specifically wrote in a "statute of limitations" on a poor man's debts. Every seventh year, Hebrew slaves were to be set free (see Exod. 21:2) and all debts were to be forgiven (see Deut. 15:1). There was even a stipulation that in the fiftieth year, all property that had been mortgaged (except houses in walled cities) was to be returned to its original owners (see Lev. 25:10).

Not lending money at interest had behind it the love of God for the poor and His desire that their poverty not lead to enslavement. It also speaks of a God who demands that we act with compassion toward those in need.

3. God demands compassion, not chastisement.

I (John) will never forget a lesson a Dallas Seminary friend, Lars Soderholm, once taught me in downtown Fort Worth, Texas. At the time, Lars was a Young Life staff person and I was a college student leading a club in town.

One day I went to his office in the heart of the business district to pick up some camp brochures and meet with Lars for lunch. It was the kind of cold day when the wind whistles down the high-rise corridors like a freight train, and all you can do is pull your coat tighter around you and quicken your pace to get inside. As we walked to lunch that way, we barreled right past one of the numerous homeless people who had taken up temporary residence in an alley.

"Hey, man . . . hey, friend . . . stop a minute, will you?" the man said. He apparently thought we had something to offer him. When we didn't stop, he began walking after us, asking us for money to get something to eat.

I was continuing my march through the cold to the restaurant when I suddenly noticed that Lars wasn't beside me anymore. I turned and saw him talking to the homeless man. "Are you really hungry?" Lars asked. "Or are you just looking for money to get a drink?"

"Oh, no sir," he said. "I'm hungry. I am."

"Then why don't you come and join us for lunch?"

I was speechless. I'd given out some change and even an occasional dollar or two to a homeless person, but never had I asked one to be a lunch guest.

"You mean it?" the man asked, apparently as shocked as I was.

"Absolutely," Lars answered. "We're treating. Let's go to that hamburger shop down the street."

The three of us walked the rest of the way to the burger place, where we stepped inside out of the cold. The waitress seated us with more than a few double takes at Lars's newfound friend. Soon we all thawed out and had hot soup, fries, and hamburgers set in front of us.

For most of the lunch, I remained quiet as Lars asked about the man's life and family and whether he had a saving faith. When it came to his salvation, he said he'd heard more sermons at the soup kitchens than any 10 churchgoers he knew. And we believed it when he went on to recite Bible verse after Bible verse from memory.

As we finished our meal, I remember two things distinctly. The first was how the man had carefully taken half his french fries and half his hamburger and pushed them aside during lunch. Now that we were leaving, he wrapped them up and put them in his coat pocket—a feast for later that day or perhaps the next. And I remember feeling ashamed of myself for my callousness, bordering on contempt, when I'd first walked past him. He was a man with a life story, what seemed like a genuine faith, and a contagious smile.

Don't get me wrong. In today's world, stopping in an alley to talk to a street person could be an invitation to disaster. But on that day, it was an opportunity for me to gain a lasting lesson in human worth and compassion.

Psalm 15 steers us toward solid ground because it challenges us to walk where God walks. And Almighty God has so much compassion that He demanded that a creditor who held a person's coat in pledge take it back to him at night so he'd have some protection from the cold (see Exod. 22:25–26).

So What Is This Verse Saying to Us Nonbankers?

Have you ever been down and vulnerable and then had someone take advantage of that fact? Instead of being people who take advantage of the poor by charging them "biting" interest on what they need to live, we should be people of love and compassion—people who care enough to give sacrificially to someone in need . . . someone like Monica.

It is my (John's) great privilege to lead a weekly men's Bible study. We now have over 100 regular attendees, and in the early days one of the most faithful was a man named Greg. He'd sit quietly in the back, yet when we'd break into small groups after the Bible lesson, he was always warm and animated. In the times I sat with him, he spoke of his love for his wife, Monica, and their two young daughters, his desire to be God's man, and his avid love of flying.

It was a beautiful spring day when I got an urgent message from another member of the group. There'd been a terrible accident. An ultralight plane had crashed, and he thought it was Greg's.

He was right. Greg had been flying when some unseen turbulence hit his tiny, homemade plane, ripping off a wing and sending him spiraling into the ground. Unfortunately, he left behind little in the way of financial help for his family.

I called Monica, and we talked and prayed over the phone. But many of us in the group wanted to do more for the family. Though we didn't know all their needs at the time, I told the men what had happened at our meeting the next week. We prayed for Greg's wife and children, and then we took up a collection. We had no specific goal or need in mind at the time, just a desire to express our love and concern in a tangible way.

Several days later, Monica called the church where we hold our meetings. Tearfully, she expressed her appreciation for the gift. Then she asked one of the pastors to please pass along how God had used it. It seems that she had just gotten the bill for Greg's funeral and burial—a bill she couldn't pay. And then she opened the envelope from the men of our group, and it covered the cost of the services, almost down to the penny.

Pure and undefiled religion is helping widows, orphans, and those in need, not charging interest to the poorest of the poor but showing compassion and care like the Lord Himself. David's challenge in Psalm 15 is for any man or woman who can, to help lift up others who can't give back—people with real needs like a homeless man in Fort Worth or Monica and her two daughters.

We've looked at nine steps that can take us to the solid ground God Himself inhabits. But there's still one more step. And interestingly, it takes us back to the first place where we're told to stand—integrity—and something to avoid ardently if we're to anchor our lives in His character.

Reflections
Financial Fairness

1. This chapter discusses the subject of not lending money at interest. After reading the chapter, what do you think that means to you?

2. Think of someone you know who acted like a loan shark. How did friends and family members view the person? What was his or her reputation?

3. Recall a situation where a poor person asked you for money. How did you respond? Why? Think about and discuss with your spouse or a friend the balance between meeting needs and protecting yourself from real dangers.

4. Have you ever been in excessive debt? If you have, did you feel you were in bondage? If you were able to pay off that debt, how did you feel afterward?

5. What could you do this week to help another person in need? Will you do it? When? How?

Chapter 17

The Tenth Key

Putting Principle Above Profit

Nor does he take a bribe against the innocent.

ince the day Jim Sutherland first set foot on a construction site, he had dreamed of owning his own construction company. Tracing all the way back to his boyhood love of erecting things, there was just something about building from the ground up—knowing *you'd* done it—that he found exciting.

During the summers in high school, he'd been on a construction crew. It was hard work, but there's no better way to learn how to build than to do it yourself. Some guys went the college route, taking architecture, construction, and design classes, but their experience in the field was limited. Jim learned it from the inside out—and never regretted the path he'd chosen.

After high school, he hired on full-time and soon became head of one of the largest framing crews in the city. Word spread quickly about the quality and speed of his work, as well as the dependability of his crew. Soon he'd brought more work to his boss's company than it could handle. When Jim saw there was more than enough work to go around, he formed a company and ventured out on his own.

Like most young companies, Jim's needed a break to get "over the hump." That's when the phone call came that changed his life. Late one afternoon, he was informed he'd been selected to submit a bid on a huge housing development the city, state, and federal governments were putting together. The next morning, he massed the troops, quickly crunched the numbers for his bid, and submitted it. After that, all he could do was wait.

Ten days later, the mayor's office called. Jim was asked to make room in his schedule for a meeting with the mayor the next afternoon. True, the job wasn't in the bag, but he felt confident a meeting with the mayor was a good sign. He also knew he would do everything he could to give his company a better-than-average chance of being selected. Landing a project like this could mean millions of dollars in revenue over the next few years. Plus, if he could deliver a first-rate product on budget and on time, the possibilities for future business could be endless.

The next afternoon, the mayor greeted Jim with a big smile and a hearty handshake. Their conversation revolved around the usual—where they were raised, family, hobbies, sports, and construction. It seemed the mayor had some experience in the field—in fact, years ago, he'd helped a college buddy start a construction firm in the Midwest. From Jim's standpoint, the conversation couldn't have been going better.

Then the mayor lit a cigar and turned to face Jim. "Jim," he said, "I know this contract is important to you. You're a good man with a good reputation. I also know what it's like to get a company off the ground. It can be nip and tuck. That's why I want to do whatever I can to help you."

"Well, thank you, sir," Jim said. "That's kind. I appreciate it."

"Step over here, my friend," the mayor continued. He pointed to a large model layout of the proposed development sprawled over a huge conference table in his office. "Just look at this thing. Green space, play areas, houses. Why, there's even going to be a community recreation center! We want this to be a model community for the entire nation. Think of it—helping families improve their standard of living, their quality of life. I just know that's something you'd want to be a part of."

"Yes, sir, it is. It's a worthy project," Jim replied.

The mayor moved toward a cabinet, opened it, and turned on his stereo, making sure the volume was up so no one outside could hear the rest of their conversation. "That's why I want to ask you to do something that will ensure the best possible success in making this a first-rate project," the mayor said.

"And what would that be?" Jim asked.

"I want you to resubmit your bid," replied the mayor. "Make it five thousand dollars higher than the original."

"I'm sorry, sir, I don't understand. Why would I do that?"

"Because," the mayor said with a glint in his eye, "I'll make sure you get the job. Then you'll keep the project at the original cost, and you and I will split the five thousand. Savvy?"

Jim couldn't believe his ears. Sure, this kind of thing happened—more often than people outside the industry imagined. But for the *mayor* to be so open and blatant about it made it seem even more unethical.

Jim looked nervously around the room, and then his eyes met the mayor's. They were studying him, watching carefully to see if he was going to play ball. The mayor sensed some hesitation on Jim's part, but rather than pressure him too much, he decided to reel him in slowly. *After all,* he thought, *this kid will never make it without a break like this. He needs it more than I do.*

The mayor smiled, put his arm around Jim's shoulders, and walked him toward the door. "Well, you think about it, son," said the mayor. "I'll wait to hear from you. But don't take too much time. Remember, there are others out there who'd just jump at a chance like this. Don't be left out of the game." With that, he opened the door and showed Jim out.

Jim walked nervously past the secretary and stood fidgeting at the elevator doors. The doors opened, and he stepped inside and plunged five floors into despair and confusion.

Have you ever faced something like that? If not, what do you think you would do in Jim's place? Just reading about it can make the decision seem easy. But in the heat of the moment, with influential people pulling the strings, big money up for grabs, and the future of your company, your family—your security—at stake, the lines between right and wrong can get blurred.

Looking Back on Bribery

That's not a new problem. God said of the people in Isaiah's day, "Your rulers are rebels, and companions of thieves; everyone loves a bribe, and chases after rewards" (Isa. 1:23). No doubt about it, accepting a bribe can make life a lot easier. It can be money for the kids' education or a new camper. It can ease the stress of a house payment or take care of an ailing parent's mounting medical bills. Bribery can enrich your lifestyle.

But it can also bankrupt your life. Ecclesiastes 7:7 says, "For oppression makes a wise man mad, and a bribe corrupts the heart." It's one of the quickest ways we know to mortgage your integrity—blinding you to what's fair and right and opening your eyes to a world that deals under the table and behind the back.

Remember the first few words of Psalm 15? "O Lord, who may abide in Thy tent? Who may dwell on Thy holy hill? *He who walks with integrity. . . .*" It's no mistake God includes that statement first, because it's the foundation for everything else in the psalm. It makes sense that as we examine the last of this list of things that a person who walks intimately with God does, we come full circle to integrity.

Before going further, it's important to define *bribe.* According to *Webster's Dictionary,* it is "money or favor given or promised in order to influence the judgment or conduct of a person in a position of trust."[1]

Time hasn't changed that a bit. The Hebrew word implies exactly the same thing: "And you shall not take a bribe, for a bribe blinds the clear-sighted and subverts the cause of the just" (Exod. 23:8). In other words, a bribe is an attempt to thwart an outcome with which God would be pleased. It takes what seems to be in a person's best interest and places it above what's best according to God.

Knowing that doesn't make the *temptation* any easier to resist, though, does it? After all, how's a little extra cash on the side going to hurt anything—especially, in a case like Jim's, when no one but the taxpayers would be hurt?

That's what Satan wants us to believe. But when we look at the Bible, we see a far different picture. There are at least three ways bribery can short-change our lives, two of which are mentioned in Exodus 23:8.

The Bite Bribery Takes

First, *accepting a bribe makes you look at the world from someone else's point of view instead of God's.* That's what it means for a bribe to "blind the clear-sighted." If we accept something of value from someone for a "favor," we oblige ourselves to live by his or her standards. What God deems best suddenly takes a back seat.

Several years ago, a friend of mine (John's) was asked to do some work for his superior—work the superior would get credit for and that would earn him an official level of recognition he didn't deserve. My friend was offered money for his effort.

I'm happy to say my friend steered clear of it, knowing it would misrepresent the situation and force him to do things his superior wanted, whether he agreed with them or not. He was wise enough to realize faithful men of God don't do that. Yes, he lost the extra income—something he could have really used at the time. But his integrity was intact. And after all, what's more important? "Better is the poor who walks in his integrity, than he who is crooked though he be rich" (Prov. 28:6).

Second, *bribery makes innocent people get the short end of the stick.* That's what "subverting the cause of the just" means. It creates a situation in which people who would have gotten a fair shake are squeezed out of the picture. It's really a form of arrogance that assumes, "What I need is more important than what you need, so I'm going to stack the deck in my favor."

A pastor friend of mine (John's) faced a situation in his church in which an injustice was done. A lot of people were hurt by it. Several members became vocal, questioning the church leadership's handling of the situation. One of the questioners was a real estate developer who had several deals in the making with one of the leaders.

In an attempt to calm the water, that leader approached the developer and gently hinted that if things didn't settle down, certain listings and pending deals might fall to someone else. But the developer wasn't willing to play ball. Despite having hundreds of thousands of dollars on the line, he refused to back down. He knew that if he did, innocent people would lose a needed spokesman. Making sure *they* got a fair shake was more important to this man than lining his pockets. He knew and believed the truth of Proverbs 21:15: "The execution of justice is joy for the righteous, but is terror to the workers of iniquity."

Third, *accepting a bribe can threaten hearth and home.* Proverbs 15:27 says, "He who profits illicitly troubles his own house, but he who hates bribes will live." In other words, if you want to make sure your home is one of stability, trust, and safety, be someone who runs from a bribe as if it were the plague.

Balaam, in the Old Testament book of Numbers, had to learn that lesson the hard way. As a prophet, he had the responsibility of accurately reporting all that God revealed to him. To do otherwise would mean trouble.

Balak was king of Moab, one of Israel's archenemies. Just before entering the promised land, Israel camped on the plains of Moab (just east of the Jordan River). When Balak saw this, he was afraid his country might be overrun. Knowing he was outnumbered, he figured the best way to defeat the Israelites was to turn God against them—and the best way to do that was to have one of God's spokesmen pronounce a curse against them. So he sent an entourage of

VIPs to Balaam, complete with a payoff, to entice him to do just that.

Balaam consulted God, who told him not to do it, so he refused. Not willing to be put off, Balak sent another group to persuade Balaam—a group more distinguished than the first. God allowed Balaam to go with them, but He was displeased Balaam *wanted* to go. That set up one of the most interesting conversations recorded in the Bible.

After Balaam had saddled his donkey and started on his way, the donkey suddenly turned from the road and headed into a field. Balaam beat her, trying his best to turn her back, but with no success. She walked to a vineyard and ended up between two walls. For no apparent reason, she pressed against one of the walls, squeezing Balaam's foot.

Once again, he struck her. She moved on, but not in the direction he wanted. She went a little farther, then suddenly lay down. By this time, Balaam was fit to be tied, so he really walloped her. Numbers 22:28–29 says, "And the LORD opened the mouth of the donkey, and she said to Balaam, 'What have I done to you, that you have struck me these three times?' Then Balaam said to the donkey, 'Because you have made a mockery of me! If there had been a sword in my hand, I would have killed you by now.'"

The donkey went on to point out that she had never behaved in a manner like this before, and she gently implied that anyone with half a lick of horse sense would realize something more than meets the eye was going on.

That's when God opened Balaam's eyes so he could see what the donkey had been seeing all along—the angel of the Lord blocking the way. Verse 32 reads, "And the angel of the Lord said to him, 'Why have you struck your donkey these three times? Behold, I have come out as an adversary, because your way was contrary to me. But the donkey saw me and turned aside from me these three times. If she had not turned aside from me, I would surely have killed you just now, and let her live.'"

Balaam realized his sin. As the apostle Peter said, he was a man who "loved the wages of unrighteousness" (2 Pet. 2:15). Fortunately, he got his act together, pronounced a blessing on Israel not once but *three* times, and forfeited the money Balak would have given him.

Though Numbers doesn't mention it, it's fair to assume Balaam had a family. If so, think about this: What if the angel had been forced to take his life? Imagine the effect that would have had on his family. His wife and children would have been left to deal with not only heartache and loneliness, but also living the rest of their lives with the stigma of a husband and father who forgot his God for a price.

Turning Away from Bribery

Jim Sutherland understood the dangers of accepting a bribe. That's why, despite the temptation to take the mayor up on his offer, he refused. Not only that, but he also contacted the FBI, which set up a sting with Jim as the primary operative and nabbed the mayor for soliciting a bribe.

What made the difference for Jim? How did he defend against the temptation to "go along to get along"? And how can you and I mount the same defense?

First, we've got to acknowledge the obvious. That is, just as we've seen, *we must realize that the cost of accepting a bribe is too high.* When we commit ourselves to a biblical perspective on the issue, that fact pops clearly into focus. It costs us our integrity, our godly perspective, our sense of justice, our safety, and the security and sanctity of our homes. Anyone who seeks to please God knows nothing is worth that.

Second, as much as possible, *we need to stay away from people who offer and accept bribes.* Paul reminded the Corinthians that "bad company corrupts good morals" (1 Cor. 15:33). We realize that, for some of you, completely isolating yourself is impossible. Your world is one of bribes and payoffs. Still, our guess is there are people of good moral character around you who will help reinforce what you believe. Spend as much time as you can with them.

Third, *if someone offers you a bribe, immediately tell a Christian you trust.* That might be a pastor, counselor, family member, or friend. Whoever it is, make sure it's someone who loves you enough to hold you accountable. If someone else knows you've been offered a bribe, you're far less likely to accept it. But temptation kept to oneself often blossoms into sin.

The Inner Reward of Honesty

Bill Remming had a first-class technological mind and a first-rate idea. For several years, he and a handful of engineers at his young company had been pioneering a new technology that would create a quantam leap in progress in his industry. After perfecting the technology itself, they worked long and hard to find the right buyer who could help them beat a path to the marketplace.

After months of searching, they came across a company that seemed a perfect fit. Dynamic, flexible, and innovative, the leadership of the company seemed interested in what Bill's company had to offer. But as is often the case, Bill hadn't been the only one working night and day. Half a dozen competitors had seen great potential in similar technology and had worked feverishly to get their ideas out as well. Four of them had also contacted the company interested in Bill's ideas.

Now the race was coming down to the wire. Bill had been informed that the choice would be made between his technology and that of a more established and well-known firm. The payoff was huge—$8 million, to be exact. This was the big leagues, and Bill knew what was at stake—the future of his company, financial security for his family, and the risk of having worked thousands of hours without a dime to show for it. The pressure was on.

Two days before the final decision, Bill received a call from the attorney who was brokering the deal. He got right to the bottom line. If Bill were willing to provide a $100,000 "finder's fee" to him, the attorney would guarantee the contract for Bill's company.

It took Bill a few seconds to respond, but his answer was decisive. "No," he said, "I don't do that kind of thing."

"Don't be foolish, Bill," said the attorney. "Understand that for a measly one hundred thousand dollars, I'm guaranteeing you eight million dollars."

"The answer is still no," said Bill, and with that he hung up the phone.

I wish we could tell you Bill got the contract anyway, but he didn't. Even worse, he had to fold the company's tents just 18 months later. But despite what it cost him in financial security, Bill knows that from God's perspective, the other guy lost out. "I can't say I wasn't tempted," he recalled later, "but I've never regretted my decision." He knew he'd have to face himself in the mirror each morning, as well as stand before God at the end of his life. Eight million dollars just wasn't worth that.

As we said at the start of the chapter, bribery can take a lot of different forms, including some that aren't even monetary. A group of friends, for instance, might "bribe" one of their number with a threatened loss of friendship if he or she doesn't drop another friend the others consider undesirable. But the end is the same. Bribery is an attempt to get people to put what seems good for themselves ahead of what God says is good. People of integrity recognize that. Armed with a clear perspective from God's Word and a conviction that doing right is more important than a fat bank account (or the wrong kind of friends), they can look a bribe square in the eyes and stare it down.

The payoff may not be in dollars and cents, but it's still priceless. When combined with the other things we've explored, it opens the door of fellowship and intimacy with God—in the words of our psalm, abiding in His tent and dwelling on His holy hill.

Our Lord wasn't willing to trade that away either. When Satan tempted Jesus in the wilderness, he offered Him more wealth and power than we can imagine. All he asked was that Christ trade the Cross for a throne and worship the enemy. Fortunately, He didn't give in. He understood far more was at stake—namely, our salvation and the glory, fellowship, and unity He had enjoyed with the Father from eternity past. No amount of fame and wealth in this life was worth losing that.

People who know the power of a bribe know that, too. Unwilling to trade fellowship with God for prestige with men, they refuse to give in to the temptation. The reward is that their sleep is sweet, their fellowship with God is deep and abiding, and their future is full of the promise of hearing, "Well done, good and faithful slave; . . . enter into the joy of your master" (Matt. 25:21).

No doubt about it—that's a deal worth living for.

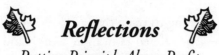

Reflections

Putting Principle Above Profit

1. In your own words, what is a bribe, and why is it wrong?

2. Imagine yourself in Bill Remming's position of being asked for a "finder's fee" by the attorney brokering a business deal. How do you think you would have responded? Why?

3. John and Rick discuss three ways in which bribery can hurt us and our loved ones. Which of those do you think represents the greatest danger? Why?

4. John and Rick also provide three suggestions for resisting the temptation to accept a bribe. Which of those do you believe would be most helpful to you? Why?

Chapter 18

"Never Be Shaken"

O ur part of this book is coming to an end.

Your part is just beginning.

Yet as we close, perhaps the best part of the entire book is left to read, ponder, and put into practice. We refer to the incredible promise from Almighty God at the end of Psalm 15: "He who does these things will never be shaken."

What a wonderful way to finish a book! That's a promise we need so much because it actually contains a double blessing. First, as we've seen, we gain personally, relationally, and spiritually when we apply the 10 principles we've learned from Psalm 15. Then, as if that's not benefit enough, we have this ironclad offer from the Lord Himself of an inner layer of stability in a shaken, changeable world.

If this sounds like something that's too good to be true, remember that Jesus made a similar promise on His last night with the disciples before the Crucifixion. He had spent three years teaching them and demonstrating every element of a life that honors the Father, and now He had just washed their feet. Then He told them plainly, "For I gave you an example that you also should do as I did to you" (John 13:15).

There's the challenge. Just like David in Psalm 15, Jesus was saying that we're called to follow a pattern of godliness. And also like David, He went on to say that there's great benefit in doing so: "If you know these things, you are blessed if you do them" (John 13:17).

That's your promise, too. As you seek to apply and live out the godly pattern put forth by David in Psalm 15—a pattern modeled to absolute perfection by the Lord Jesus—your life will be blessed. There are no ifs, ands, or buts—just the rock-solid certainty that you're building an unshakable foundation that can weather any storm and outlast any season of testing or trial.

Moving into Action

It's your time to build a life that reflects integrity and dependability, to build a life that rests on stability and solid ground, to build a life with the 10 precut stones that you can pick up in Psalm 15.

You can begin to fit them into your life by memorizing Psalm 15. Review chapter 11, and take some advice from Dave Hopkins that helped so many summer staffers at Forest Home. The time you'll invest in planting Psalm 15 in your mind and heart will be the best preparation you can make for a time when the paper-thin world we live on begins to shake.

Some doubt that a "big one" is really coming in each person's life. But it is. It may be cancer, a car wreck, a bad business decision, or some other unforeseen disaster. But when it happens—as it happened with King David—it won't cause you to trip and fall out of control.

In fact, David told us, "The steps of a man are established by the LORD; and He delights in his way. When he falls, he shall not be hurled headlong; because the LORD is the One who holds his hand" (Ps. 37:23–24). When trials come, He'll be holding your hand.

Picture a dad holding his toddler's hand while the child is learning to walk. Dad knows that the learning process will involve some tumbles, so he holds on to prevent a total, nose-scraping wipeout. Though the child trips, he doesn't actually hit the ground, because Dad holds him securely.

In a real sense, Psalm 15 allows us to take our heavenly Father's hand and keep hold of it so we can walk without falling.

Are you ready to take that journey? Can your life benefit from a direct dose of godly character? Will your life look any different, and will others notice? Is it possible for others to see Jesus in the way you live?

The truths in Psalm 15 may not all come together in your life overnight. But each has the power to change you for the better from the inside out.

Joining the All-Stars!

Wouldn't it be great to go back to biblical times and visit with the all-star heroes whose lives were personally touched by God? Did you know that applying those 10 traits in Psalm 15 puts you in their league?

Look at any of those people of faith and see how the principles you've learned from Psalm 15 are reflected in their actions and choices. We might start in the wilderness with Moses and Aaron, who trusted God—even when it was tremendously difficult.

Or look in on Joseph in Egypt and his life of seamless integrity. We could get our hands dirty by working righteousness with Nehemiah, or we could meditate on the deep things of God like Job and Jeremiah.

We could travel a dusty road with a good-hearted Samaritan and see first-hand how he did good, not harm, to a neighbor in need. We might observe Jonathan's amazing loyalty as he refused to embrace his father's hatred of his best friend and "take up a reproach against him," in spite of the fact that doing so would cost him his inheritance.

We could even visit with Timothy and hear him honor his godly mother and grandmother, who modeled their faith before him, taught him God's Word, and stood behind him in prayer as he lived the faith he learned from them and pastored a church in Ephesus.

We might find ourselves sitting on the threshing floor, reflecting with Ruth on how much easier it would have been for her to have stayed in her own country; but having made a commitment, she didn't walk away from it. She stayed with her mother-in-law, and God provided. Or how about tagging along with Zaccheus and watching the amazement on the faces of those he had "charged excessive interest" as he paid back the money he owed them. We could listen in on James's exhortation to his church not to grant special privileges to those they perceived as well-to-do over those of lesser means. And, of course, we could look at the life of the Lord Jesus, who demonstrated all 10 traits to perfection.

What a hall-of-fame lineup in that list of great saints and our Savior! But that kind of rock-solid life wasn't just for them. It's for all of us, each and every day.

Psalm 15 isn't merely a list of things to do in order to gain God's approval. It describes what true Christian character looks like in action. Living it out doesn't make us immune to life-shaking experiences. But when the unwanted and unexpected happen, God promises we won't be shaken.

God has given us 10 steps to follow. It's our prayer that as you take each one, your own character will become a clear image of Christ's and a wonderful blessing to your family and those around you.

John Trent

Rick Hicks

Appendix:
Resources
to Reinforce an
Unshakable Life

Now that you've looked at Psalm 15's 10 keys to an unshakable lifestyle and done some self-evaluation, you may want to concentrate on certain areas and do further study. To help you, we've listed additional resources below that expand on the principles in the psalm and can guide you further down the road toward the solid ground of godly character. The list isn't exhaustive, but it will give you a good place to start.

The resources are grouped according to the three divisions of the 10 keys, although some of the books obviously cover a broader scope than the section in which we've put them.

Anchoring Our Personal Lives:

Walking with Integrity; Working Righteousness; Speaking the Truth

Charles Swindoll, *Integrity: The Mark of Godliness* (Multnomah, 1981).
Charles Swindoll, *Three Steps Forward, Two Steps Back* (Thomas Nelson, 1985).

Ken Gire, *Intimate Moments with the Savior* (Zondervan, 1990).
Greg Laurie, *The Great Compromise* (Word, 1994).
W. Phillip Keller, *The High Cost of Holiness* (Harvest House, 1988).
J.I. Packer, *A Passion for Faithfulness* (Crossway, 1995).
Jim Toombs, *Confessions of a Struggling Christian* (Multnomah, 1993).
"The Topical Memory System" (The Navigators).

Protecting Our Most Important Relationships:
Avoiding Slander; Not Doing Evil; Not Taking Up a Reproach

R. Kent Hughes, *Disciplines of a Godly Man* (Crossway, 1991).
Charles Swindoll, *Strengthening Your Grip* (Word, 1982).
Les Carter and Frank Minirth, *The Anger Workbook* (Thomas Nelson, 1993).
M. Scott Peck, *People of the Lie* (Simon & Schuster, 1983).

Guiding Our Public Walk:
Honoring the Godly; Keeping Promises; Financial Fairness

A.W. Tozer, *The Man Who Met God* (Christian Publications, 1986).
Dave Dravecky with Tim Stafford, *Comeback* (HarperCollins/Zondervan, 1990).
Elisabeth Elliot, *Shadow of the Almighty* (HarperCollins, 1958).
Stuart Briscoe, *David: A Heart for God* (Victor, 1984).
Seven Promises of a Promise Keeper, by various authors (Focus on the Family, 1994).
Daniel Busby et al., *The Christian's Guide to Worry-Free Money Management* (Zondervan, 1994).
Ron Blue, *Master Your Money* (Thomas Nelson, 1986).
Larry Burkett, *Using Your Money Wisely* (Moody, 1990).
Larry Burkett, *Debt-Free Living* (Moody, 1989).

Many of the books listed above are also available on cassette tapes.

Notes

chapter 2

1. "Roosevelt Says 'Old Ship of State Is On Same Course,' " *New York Times*, March 5, 1938.

chapter 4

1. R.W. White, "Self-Concept in School Adjustment," *Personnel and Guidance Journal*, vol. 46, 1976, pp. 478-81.

2. Quoted in J.J. Stewart Perowne, *The Book of Psalms*, vol. 1 (Grand Rapids, Mich.: Zondervan, 1966), p. 187.

chapter 6

1. Victor Hamilton, "Shakan," in Jack P. Lewis, ed., *Theological Wordbook of the Old Testament*, vol. 2 (Grand Rapids, Mich.: Eerdmans, 1972), p. 925.

chapter 7

1. *Webster's Seventh New Collegiate Dictionary* (Springfield, Mass.: Merriam-Webster, 1967).

chapter 9

1. While Rick would never brag about Forest Home, I (John) don't have to restrict my praise! Forest Home is one of the top Christian family

and youth camps in the country. My family and I have been there several times. We all appreciate the loving staff, the beautiful trees, and the commitment to biblical teaching. The kids also love the merry-go-round, Cindy loves the huge bookstore, and I love the climbing wall and outdoor adventure. For information on this camp or another outstanding Christian family camp in your area—such as Pine Cove, Mount Hermon, Word of Life, Hume Lake, Glorietta, and many others—contact Christian Camping International/USA, P.O. Box 62189, Colorado Springs, CO 80962, (719) 260-9400.

2. For more details on image management, see chapter 9 in John Trent's book *LifeMapping*, from Focus on the Family Publishing.

chapter 10

1. J.I. Packer, *Knowing God* (Downers Grove, Ill.: InterVarsity, 1973), pp. 18-19.

chapter 13

1. C.F. Keil and F. Delitzsch, *Commentary on the Old Testament*, vol. 5, "Psalms" by F. Delitzsch (Grand Rapids, Mich.: Eerdmans, reprinted 1980), p. 213.

chapter 14

1. Morris Massey, *The People Puzzle* (Reston, Va.: Reston Publishing Co., 1979), part 3.

chapter 16

1. For a more detailed look at how ancient Israel and its neighboring nations dealt with loans and interest, see the following sources: John Sutherland, "Usury: God's Forgotten Doctrine," *Crux*, March 1982, pp. 9-12; E. Neufeld, "The Rate of Interest and the Text of Nehemiah 5:11," *The Jewish Quarterly Review*, vol. XLIV, 1953-54, pp. 194-204; and E. Neufeld, "The Prohibitions Against Loans at Interest in Ancient Hebrew Laws," *Hebrew Union College Annual*, vol. XXVI, 1955, pp. 355-412.

2. Quoted in Robert Maloney, "The Teaching of the Fathers on Usury," *Vigiliae Christianae*, vol. 27, no. 4, 1973, pp. 241-65.

chapter 17

1. *Merriam-Webster's Collegiate Dictionary*, 10th ed. (Springfield, Mass.: Merriam-Webster, 1993), p. 142.

Also by John Trent, Ph.D.!

LifeMapping

This revolutionary biblical guide will enable you to leave behind the things that hold you back and make tracks in a positive new direction. Whether it's obtaining a closer relationship with God, healing the past, or overcoming bad habits, you *can* reach your desired destination! Also available on audiocassette.

The Hidden Value of a Man

The role of men in the family has become confused. This outstanding best-seller from the team of Gary Smalley and John Trent, Ph.D., helps men understand how they can develop closer, more meaningful relationships with their wives and children. Expanded paperback includes study guide!

The Language of Love

This best-seller co-written with Gary Smalley shows how to unlock communication stalemates through emotional word pictures. Thought-provoking exercises help readers understand their personality types and those of people around them. Expanded paperback includes study guide!

The Two Sides of Love

Gary Smalley and John Trent, Ph.D., show why some personalities conflict while others naturally complement one another. This paperback includes personality tests, practical counsel, and helpful study guide! Also available on audiocassette.

Available at your favorite Christian bookstore.

PUBLISHING